EVERTON STRANGE BUT BLUE

MOMENTS THAT SHOCKED AND SURPRISED THE FANS

Written by Gavin Buckland

Sport Media
A Trinity Mirror Business

Acknowledgements

Books are real team efforts, and this one would not have been possible without the great help of all those at Sport Media, especially James Cleary. A big thank you also to Dave Prentice for writing the Foreword. I would also like to thank Billy Smith, John Keith, Mark Nicholas, Eddie Holmes, Billy Butler, Michael Joyce (author of *Football League Players' Records 1888-1939*) and Tony Matthews.

Gavin Buckland

Sport Media
A Trinity Mirror Business

Published in Great Britain in 2007 & 2008 by:
Trinity Mirror Sport Media,
PO Box 48, Old Hall Street,
Liverpool L69 3EB

Executive Editor: KEN ROGERS
Art Editor: RICK COOKE
Editorial Assistant: JAMES CLEARY

ISBN 978-1905-26621-0

Printed and finished by Brolink

Foreword

You can't miss Gavin Buckland - he's tall, dark and instantly recognisable. And while he usually sits on the front row of the Goodison press box, at half-time he'll be the man surrounded by struggling hacks, especially when a match is a dour stalemate and there's no prospect of an angle on the horizon.

You see, Gav is a statistician, and he can usually be relied upon to produce an entertaining angle, statistic or snippet from even the dullest of clashes. Five disallowed goals, a Goodison riot, fireworks at the Bridge, they're all contained in the following, outrageously entertaining 230 pages or so. You see, these kind of titbits are manna from heaven when you're struggling for a line from a goalless draw with Fulham. "Ah yes, but did you know Fulham were the opposition in the most one-sided match in Everton history..." I do now. And the tale of the 'match of the century' is highly entertaining.

This is the kind of book you'll sit down to have a flick through, and still be sat down two-and-a-half hours later, pausing every few seconds only to tell anyone in earshot: "Did you know that...?" For example. Who scored the last FA Cup penalty against Everton at Goodison Park? The answer will amaze you. But you'll have to read on to find out. It's hard work unearthing these titbits. But they are literary gold.

I've written historical books myself – so know from grim experience the giddy sensation of sitting in front of micro-film machines watching adverts for Bovril and Chelsea Dubbin' whizz past your eyes eventually giving you motion sickness. But Gavin's dogged. And his research has been exhaustive. He has trawled ageing national newspaper reports and my own newspaper, the *Liverpool Echo* (although happily I'm not so old yet that any of mine appear). And this book is evidence it has been richly worthwhile.

So, in summary then: Gav is a statto, but he doesn't wear an anorak. And while there are lies, damned lies...and statistics, which can put even the most unbelievable of tall-stories in the shade. Did you know Everton once scored eight at Anfield (and yes, Liverpool were in residence at the time) and have won more league games against the Reds on their own ground than any other team. Don't believe me? Then read on. But be warned. Once you've started you'll find it hard to put down...but you'll have a fund of entertaining tales to relate next time you pop into your local. And if no-one believes them, you've got the written evidence here in your hands.

David Prentice,
Chief sports writer, *Liverpool Echo*

Contents

Contents

Neville Southall shows his outfield credentials during an Everton pre-season game in Wales, 1993

Introduction

One dictionary definition of 'strange' is 'being definitely out of the ordinary and unexpected; slightly odd or even a bit weird.' Well *Everton: Strange But Blue* unearths 50 Everton matches and incidents in other games involving the club that fit into this category.

The matches and events chosen fall into several distinct groups. Some were naturals, their presence in the forefront of the club's history being based purely on the fact they are out-of-the-ordinary. The trip to Spurs in 1958 resulted in one of the most famous league games of all time, as did the fixture against Leeds at Goodison six years later, for entirely different reasons. But others, such as the 1959 Liverpool Senior Cup final at Anfield, are not so well known.

Other encounters were included on the basis that individually they were characterized by the occurrence of several unrelated but unusual events, such as the 1979 October derby at Anfield. Other games individually feature plenty of disallowed goals, own goals and a British record for bookings (Chelsea, 1974). The full story of Sam Chedgzoy's infamous corner-kick at Goodison in 1924 is told in its entirety for the first time.

One of the by-products of the selection is that it has brought to life several matches that until now have been hidden away in the record books, such as the 2-1 win over Swansea in 1952.

The enormous archive of the *Liverpool Daily Post & Echo* were the prime source of research, as were the national newspaper archives at Manchester Central Library. A chance to view the old editions of *Athletic News* from over 100 years ago could not be turned down. The national reports were particularly interesting, and uncovered such gems as the *Sunday Times* fixation with 1970s full-back, John McLaughlin.

As well as the 50 games, there are also separate features on events such as unexpected pitch invaders, strange starts and Everton outfielders as goalkeepers. Some unique statistics are shown to put some games into context (all are correct at December 1st, 2006). The final game is certainly the most unusual I have seen – against Blackburn in 2006. But we start by going back to 1888 and Everton's eighth-ever league fixture – and who is that mysterious player appearing for Derby County?

Gavin Buckland

Harbouring a player

A unique appearance
Everton 6-2 Derby County
First Division, 27th October, 1888

There are 38,000 players who have appeared in league football since 1888. All can be accounted for in terms of clubs, appearances and goals. But, until recent years, there was one whose details remained unknown: a man of mystery who played at Anfield against Everton for Derby County, in only the second month of the League's inaugural season.

This was the reverse fixture, as the away team had beaten Everton 4-2 at the County Ground the week before. County had made a dreadful start to the season and had lost five of their first seven matches. Problems arose when they arrived in the city without three senior players, with rumours abounding of player unrest. Although two could be replaced, Derby were still one short just before kick-off when they were loaned a player at wing-half known only at the time as 'Harboard.' The Derby official history states: 'Nothing is known of Harboard and even the spelling is in doubt.'

Everton were unchanged for the encounter, and in goal they had Bob Smalley – a man who many years later would have to act as an unexpected replacement in an Everton game himself.

The game went according to the form line in front of a large crowd, for the time, of just over 5,000, although the visitors struck the first blow when Needham slotted home after just three minutes. The home team regained the ascendancy with Edgar Chadwick and centre-half Nick Ross – the best player in England at the time – both going close. Ross, who could play literally anywhere, then moved to centre-forward and equalised with a powerful shot past Marshall. The home side went 2-1 ahead shortly after with a goal from the Scot, Alex McKinnon. After 'skirmishing ensued in the visitors' half', with the 'Everton men frequently putting the Derby goal in jeopardy', Watson put the home side 3-1 up just before the interval. The contemporary newspaper reports mentioned Harboard very little, so it is assumed his contribution was minimal.

The sides changed ends immediately at half-time but the pattern of play remained unchanged, with constant Everton pressure occasionally interrupted by spirited breaks by the visitors. After Marshall had saved from Jimmy Costley, he was powerless to stop McKinnon from adding a fourth. A couple of minutes later it was 5-1, and it was Ross again with his second of the day, a stunning strike just inside the far post. Although Derby displayed great courage they were completely under the cosh, with a constant stream of corners threatening their goal. It was no surprise that a sixth was scored and it was a moment for the history books, McKinnon beating Marshall to complete his hat-trick, the first recorded by an Everton player in the league.

Although Derby fought well and grabbed a goal through Plackett near the end, they were completely outclassed by an exceptional performance by the home side. Everton had scored ten goals against County in just eight days – although more would be scored in just one game the following season, when Everton beat them 11-2 in the FA Cup, to record what is still their biggest victory in a first-team match.

POSTSCRIPT:

Everton were to have a disappointing opening campaign, fading to finish eighth in a 12-strong league. A major contributing factor was an argument that took place before the game at Blackburn, some weeks after the Derby match. Following a heated discussion over team selection policy, Alex McKinnon refused to play and moved on shortly after. The club failed to find a suitable replacement and fortunes went downhill from then on, with just eight points being gathered from the final 13 league matches.

But what about the mysterious opponent? It was not really surprising that 'Harboard' made little or no contribution to the match, as recent research has established that the anonymous wing-half was, in fact, an Everton player! His real name was actually H. Harbour, a reserve regular who did not appear in the first team but was with the club for several years. Why he was chosen in particular to start in the Derby line-up against his own club is unknown, although in the early years of league football the rules governing eligibility were more liberal than today. It is the only occurrence in league history of a player appearing for the opposition against his own club, other than when being officially on loan. In subsequent seasons the rules were tightened up when players failed to attend, with Everton being the beneficiaries on one occasion (see below).

Other non-appearances

Bill Richards, West Brom, 29th September, 1894

There are 26 occasions in league history when teams fielded less than 11 men due to players failing to turn up. This was one of them. The prolific forward missed the train from the Midlands for the match at Goodison Park, which meant that their opponents started the game with just ten men. The home side romped to a 4-1 victory, with the *Liverpool Echo* reporting that his absence, 'undoubtedly robbed the match of much interest.'

The crowd, 25th March 1899

The final Saturday of the month was not only Grand National day, but it also brought rotten weather to the North West when Everton were due to play at Preston in a friendly. On arrival at Deepdale they were greeted by driving rain and howling winds. When the great rivals took to the pitch at half past three the crowd numbered just six. Yes, just six spectators for a game between two of the game's superpowers - all having travelled up from Liverpool for the fixture. Having looked at the size of the 'crowd' officials from both clubs decided to abandon the contest. 'It was keenly disappointing for the few enthusiasts who had journeyed to Preston', was the *Daily Post's* rather understated view.

The referee, 16th March 1901

In the early years of the 20th century arguments between officials and the footballing authorities over money meant that it was not unusual for officials to fail to turn up for matches. For the home match against Stoke City, the referee Mr Adams did not arrive and was replaced by Mr Forsbet. After discussion between the clubs it was decided that the fixture should retain league status.

A linesman, 7th January 1911

The linesman for the Toffees match at Preston failed to attend, but strangely he was replaced by Bob Smalley, the former Everton goalkeeper. Smalley had become an accountant after his career ended and coincidentally had played in the match against Derby in 1888, which featured the imposter, 'Harboard.'

The Manchester City train, 15th September 1928

The train failed to turn up in Manchester for the City players and consequently they arrived only ten minutes before the kick-off at Goodison, having changed in taxis on the way to the ground. Despite (or maybe because of) this unusual preparation they romped to a 6-2 win with Tommy Johnson, later to win league and FA Cup medals with the Toffees, netting five of them.

The match ball, 2nd September 1933

A truly comical moment at Birmingham City. The players and officials lined up for the start of the second half but then realised there was no match ball! A frantic search ensued and after a couple of minutes it turned up under a disused chair. How and why it got there was unknown.

A linesman, 20th August 1955

Preston run riot at Goodison on the opening day in a 4-0 victory that featured Tom Finney's 100th league goal. But that was nothing against the odd tannoy announcement prior to the game: 'Will any qualified linesman or referee please report to the club office.' At that point several volunteer spectators invaded the pitch and, despite the attentions of the police, a couple disappeared down the players' tunnel only to return to the stands when the match officials finally turned up. A 1980 Central League game at Goodison was also interrupted when the PA system announced if the owner of a car, which was causing an obstruction, could please move it. The only problem was that it belonged to George Wood, who was playing for Everton on the pitch at the time.

Who was Harbour?

The 1901 census has two H. Harbours, and it is likely that the player in this match was Henry W. Harbour, then aged 33, who was living in Cheshire.

His appearance for the opposition is without precedent in league history. There are only two similar occurrences – the first was in 1924-25, when Albert Pape arrived with the Orient team to play at Manchester United and was promptly signed by United and appeared for them in the match. As a result of this the transfer deadline rule was introduced.

When New Brighton arrived at Hartlepools United (as they were then known) with nine players in 1946-47, the New Brighton manager Neil McBain (a former Everton player) played in goal and became the oldest-ever Football League player at 51. The other place was taken by Nicholas Evans, son of a Hartlepools director, though he was not strictly a player with the home team.

George Wood - Being beaten by Mick Lyons in the Anfield derby of 1979 (see Match 39). He also caused an obstruction during a Central League encounter a year later

A trio of keepers

All-change between the posts
Sheffield United 4-2 Everton
First Division, 26th February, 1895

In the era of multiple substitutes, one particular aspect of the game that has largely disappeared for good is that of the outfielder as goalkeeper. The last occasion a Blues outfielder took over between the sticks was at Stamford Bridge in 1985, when Kevin Ratcliffe replaced the dismissed Neville Southall (see Match 42). The Everton captain did not concede, but the sight of a defender or forward putting on the gloves often led to some memorable and amusing moments – hence the number of games featured in this book where it happened at some point.

The 1890s were very much like the 1970s in many respects for Everton, symbolized by several near-misses in the league and FA Cup. Season 1894-95 was no different, a campaign that would see the club eventually finish second to Sunderland. Luck (and as it turned out, goalkeepers) were in short supply when Everton travelled to Yorkshire with seven games left in the season, aiming to pull back a two-point deficit at the top. The two clubs had met a month earlier at Goodison, with a goal from McInnes stealing a point for the home team.

It was very much a patched-up team that journeyed on the morning of the game, accompanied by a large army of supporters. Defender Bob Kelso carried a troublesome arm injury and centre-half John Holt was suffering from an injured knee while Tommy McInnes was also unwell. Although it was a holiday in Sheffield, there were barely 10,000 present when the game commenced under leaden skies and a stiff breeze.

The away fans had to wait a minute before raising the first cheers of the day. Straight from the start Milward played the ball to McMillan, whose cross was met perfectly by McInnes who shot in off the post. The subsequent quarter of an hour saw continuous pressure from Everton, with John Bell (twice) and Boyle forcing the legendary Blades keeper, Bill 'Fatty' Foulke, into action. However, even Foulke was unable to prevent Abe Hartley adding a second goal.

It was at this point that things took a turn for the worse, for a goalmouth scramble saw the Everton goalkeeper Dick Williams make a great save from the United forward, Jimmy Yates, only to have his leg trodden on by the opposing player. Williams bravely continued for a few minutes, but according to *Athletic News*: 'His injury was not only a danger to himself but also the fortunes of his team', and he was carried off by four team-mates.

A strange decision was made: Bob Kelso, whose injured arm cast a doubt on his presence on the day, was amazingly picked to go between the sticks. Although he did well, making a couple of good stops, he flayed at a long shot and from the rebound was powerless to prevent Harry Hammond pulling a goal back for the home team. Just before half-time Yates crossed in well and Hammond equalized following an astute lay-off by Davies.

At half-time Everton saw the error of their ways, and forward Alf Milward went in goal with Kelso returning to his usual position of full-back. Remarkably this was the third stopper used by the visitors in the game. The 10 men of Everton continued to fight manfully and the early exchanges in the second period were even, with Bell and McInnes again going close and Docherty hitting the post for United. Milward was being kept busy in the Everton goal, and at one point saved no less than six shots in a five-minute spell.

Bad luck continued to plague Everton, and 15 minutes from time Hammond completed his hat-trick with a goal from what looked a suspiciously offside position. Although the visitors fought back desperately to keep their title hopes alive, Foulke was proving a tough obstacle to beat and a clear penalty was denied when McInnes was upended in the box. The afternoon was perfectly summed up when Milward saved cleanly only to be bundled over the line (with the ball) for the fourth goal. The *Daily Post's* comment that referee Pennington 'gave anything but satisfaction' was about as critical as newspapers got in those days.

POSTSCRIPT:

The final score was 4-2 and Everton failed to bridge the gap at the top, finishing five points behind the Wearsiders. It was an eventful and controversial game, and it remains the only first-team match in which Everton have used three goalkeepers.

Only one other match played by the club has featured three keepers playing for the Blues – a friendly against South Africa at Goodison in October 1958, just three days before the debacle against Spurs (see Match 25). After 41 minutes of the first half, with the score at 4-0 to Everton, Jimmy O'Neill suffered a reoccurrence of a knee injury and was carried off. That great joker Brian Harris replaced him, and entertained the crowd by deliberately straying outside of the area so they could wave him back. After 12 minutes of amusing antics in the home goal, Albert Dunlop replaced Harris and then let in four goals in the second period – a good warm-up for the weekend as it happened. Incidentally, Everton ran out 7-4 winners.

Bramall Lane obviously possesses a bit of voodoo for Everton keepers. In October 1920 our trusted custodian, Tom Fern, fell to the ground after injuring a shoulder and, despite lying there helpless, the match continued and United's Fred Brown took advantage and scored. Defender Tom Fleetwood went in goal for the 15 minutes that Fern was off the pitch. Feigning injury is supposed to be a curse of the modern game, but it has been prevalent for longer than you think, and steps have been previously been taken to tackle the problem before. The *Liverpool Echo's* comments on Fern's honesty are illuminating: 'Of course, in the bad old days a player went down injured to force a stoppage. Now there is little of that sharp practice.'

Tom Fleetwood - An Everton goalkeeper for 15 minutes against Sheffield United

A riotous assembly

Football hooliganism 19th century style
Everton 1-0 Small Heath
Match abandoned: 37 minutes
First Division, 28th December, 1895

Crowd unrest is not a recent phenomenon. Even during the inaugural league season in 1888 there were reports of trouble in an Everton game at Wolves. But the first really serious outbreak, at Goodison anyway, occurred on the final Saturday of 1895 against Small Heath (now Birmingham City).

But before looking into the trouble at that game it is worth rewinding the clock back 12 months before, to 24th December 1894 in fact, and a home game against Stoke City. Then the howling gale, driving rain and sleet turned the fixture into something close to a farce. The home team had started the game well and their constant pressure was rewarded when Richard Boyle's long-range shot arrowed past Clawley in the Stoke goal.

But after 30 minutes, with the pitch and conditions becoming increasingly unplayable, the referee Mr Brodie called the players together and decided to abandon the game. The 3,000 crowd were not exactly enamoured with this decision, and immediately vented their frustration by gathering in front of the club secretary's office, demanding their hard-earned money back with several invading the enclosure behind. Wisely Mr Brodie explained his decision to the angry mob and a further address, to appease the crowd, was made by the Everton chairman, George Mahon, who announced something rather unusual. After abandoning the game, the referee would now take charge of a friendly! Why it was decided that the conditions were reasonable for a friendly, and not a first-team game, were never explained. Everton won 2-1 and then won the replayed league fixture two weeks later by the comfortable margin of 3-0.

And so to the events of a year later. The home team headed into the match as firm favourites, leading the table while their opponents languished at the bottom. Everton had also won two and drawn one of the three matches played so far between the sides, scoring 12 goals in the process. The weather was as dire as the Stoke match. The heavy rain had caused pools of water to form in some areas of the pitch whilst the recent freezing conditions had left it rock hard in others. The poor attendance of 6,000 was in stark contrast to the 30,000 gate for the visit of Aston Villa seven days before.

Referee Mr West inspected the pitch five minutes before the start and surprisingly decided it playable, much to the chagrin of the local press: 'Altogether with the abominable state of the ground, the drenching rain, it can be imagined that it was not a pleasant game to witness.'

Johnny Holt returned to the starting line-up for the home side who started the game brightly, Milward and Chadwick combining well on the left, and the latter's cross was met by John Cameron who teed John Bell up to score. From early on it was clear that the pitch would be tricky to play on, or in the *Daily Post's* words: 'The ground was in a dreadful condition, the players slipping and floundering about in all directions whilst it was absolutely impossible to pass the ball (with) any degree of accuracy.'

Everton continued to press, with Tommy McInnes and Alf Milward both shooting straight at Roach in the 'Heathens' goal. But after 37 minutes, the referee called the players together and, despite their protestations to the contrary, walked all the participants off the pitch. There was then much confusion as officials from both clubs pressurised him to change his mind, and the point was made that he could at least have deferred making the decision to half-time. Mr West relented and the decision was made to continue the game. There was just one problem though - the players were now ensconced in the warmth of the communal baths and were not exactly keen on being subjected to the brutish elements especially (as it was reasonably argued) when they had made the offer to continue originally and it had been refused.

After 90 minutes of negotiations, when it became clear that the game would not continue – it was one of three abandoned out of six games in the First Division that day – the crowd decided to riot. The catalyst was one irate spectator who ran on the pitch to protest and was apprehended with some force by the local constabulary. Most of the spectators behind both goals then invaded the playing area and gathered around the directors' box, whilst a small number of young boys started their own game on the pitch, as if to prove a point to the match officials. Most of the crowd wanted their money back: 'One cannot help feeling some sympathy with the spectators, to many of whom the nimble sixpence is a fair sum,' was the *Liverpool Echo's* view.

The angry mob started throwing stones and other debris, with a large number of windows and the ground clock being smashed. Many also invaded the premises and caused substantial damage to club offices. The police fought a gallant rearguard action and after an hour the crowd thankfully dispersed, with several arrests.

POSTSCRIPT:

The club got panned in the press afterwards, especially as at that time there was no provision to refund spectators for a match that was not completed. The *Liverpool Echo* also pointed out that the failure to address the crowd, which had been successful 12 months before against Stoke, had also led to the unrest. Incidentally, Everton won the replayed game 3-0 two months later.

There must have been something about Christmas time in the 1890s causing crowd disruption, for on Boxing Day 1899 there was another crowd riot at the Hawthorns in the West Brom v Everton clash, when the referee ordered police into the crowd to restore order after they had been incensed by a linesman's decision.

Fed to the Wolves

The 1895-96 season saw its fair share of crowd violence. Three months before the riot against Small Heath there was an equally volatile encounter against Wolves at Molineux. With the game finely balanced at 2-2 and with five minutes left, the home team had a clearly offside goal disallowed, only to see the Toffees go up the other end and score the winner through Tommy McInnes. 'The decision seemed to incense the spectators,' according to the *Daily Post*, with the crowd making for referee Mr Armitt, at the final whistle. 'Earth, stones and other missiles were being hurled at him' before he found sanctuary in the last place you would expect to welcome a referee: the press box!

Eventually he was allowed to leave the ground safely, but not before the home support had tried to attack the Everton players as they left the ground, but fortunately none were hurt.

Cup final ball stabbed!

A 50-year who-dunnit
Aston Villa 3-2 Everton
FA Cup final, 10th April, 1897

Forget 2006 and, if you excuse the heresy, the 1966 match. The Cup final involving a Merseyside club that was characterised by the highest level of sustained excitement and quality of play is the 1897 clash between the league champions, Aston Villa, and Everton, who were aiming to lift the trophy for the first time. But the real story was the peculiar passage of the matchball following the end of the match, but much more of that later.

This was a classic encounter, rightly regarded as the best final before the move to Wembley in 1923 and, such was the enthusiasm of the crowd, many rushed onto the pitch as the players tried to leave the playing area and had to be restrained by the police. And that was only at half-time! The final took place on the 60th year of Queen Victoria's reign and *Athletic News* was effusive in its praise of the match: 'The Diamond Jubilee Cup final was in every sense a record. A bigger crowd or a better game have never been seen.'

The two clubs were regarded as the major superpowers of the game, an opinion endorsed by the *Liverpool Echo* in the lead-up to the encounter: 'The final is this year invested with exceptional attractiveness for the two clubs concerned are rightly considered the finest organisations in the country.' Villa were shortly to clinch their third title in four seasons and although Everton had finished in mid-table, they possessed some of the finest talents to play for the club in the 19th century. The goalscoring prowess of the Scot, John Bell, and his partners in a formidable forward line, Alf Milward and Edgar Chadwick. At the back were hardmen Johnny Holt and Richard Boyle, and add into the mix the versatility of one the club's greatest-ever players, Jack Taylor, and a six-game losing streak in the league prior to the final is perplexing to say the least. Coincidentally Bell, Chadwick and Holt had played in the England v Scotland match at the Palace seven days before.

Everton had reached the final by overcoming Burton Wanderers, Bury and Blackburn before defeating Derby County rather fortuitously in front of a ground-record gate of 30,000 at the Victoria Ground, Stoke. The highlight of Villa's run was a clinical 3-0 despatching of Liverpool in the semi-final. Everton had also defeated Manchester City in the Lancashire Cup final, prior to departing north to Lytham in order to prepare for the game. Percy M. Young, in his masterful history 'Football on Merseyside', published in 1963, takes up the story of this unorthodox arrangement:

'They lived modestly, and the atmosphere in their boarding house, where their manners were regarded as exemplary by other, more bourgeois residents, was friendly.'

After leaving Lytham, Everton's whereabouts for the 48 hours before kick-off were mysterious, until they turned up at a hotel in Crystal Palace, late on the day before the final. Bizarrely the first sighting of their opponents on the Saturday was at the breakfast table, as Villa had coincidentally booked into the same accommodation.

The Crystal Palace Sports Arena was overflowing for the titanic clash, with many fans breaking through the police cordon around the ground. 'Every coign of vantage was seized', said the *Liverpool Echo*, which pointed out that 'the trees which fringe the side opposite were being occupied by adventurous and enthusiastic spirits.' The *Birmingham Daily Post* painted a more dramatic picture: 'The greatest assemblage that ever attended a fixture of the kind in this or perhaps any other country.' The gate was given officially as a world-record 65,891 spectators, although there were probably many more in attendance (it was also reported that 2,000 journalists and writers were covering the game). In contrast the England game the week before had brought in only 37,000.

Villa were buoyed by the news that England international Jimmy Crabtree was passed fit before the start, which added to general feeling that the Midlands side were the favourites. Ten minutes before kick-off the Everton side took to the pitch to the delight of the crowd, who repeated their cheers when Villa entered the playing area three minutes later.

Both teams made their intentions clear from the start: no feeling out the opposition early on, the game would be about out-an-out attack. The first half especially is regarded as perhaps the finest opening 45 minutes in Cup final history. Everton started strongly with Chadwick, Milward and Abe Hartley all threatening the Villa goal. 'The play was fast and furious,' according to the

Liverpool Echo, with 'both teams doing their utmost to gain the advantage.'

Enormous kicks by the Everton full-back, Peter Meehan, were causing the Villa defence no end of problems, but at the other end John Campbell, who had already spurned two opportunities, put Villa a goal up from fully 25 yards out following good work by Athersmith and Devey. That was after 16 minutes and although the favourites had gained the upper hand, their lead lasted just five minutes, Bell finishing with typical élan after sidestepping Howard Spencer and drawing Jimmy Whitehouse from the Villa goal.

It was now Everton's turn to dominate and when Richard Boyle crossed into the goalmouth, a difficult ball was turned into his own net by the luckless Spencer, although officially Boyle is credited with the goal. They had turned a one-goal deficit into a 2-1 lead in just five minutes. But the drama in this extraordinary half was certainly not finished. Straight from the kick-off Villa were awarded a free-kick near the Everton goal, and after two crosses had been cleared Frank Wheldon put Villa back on level terms again. At 2-2 the 'excitement was now more intense than ever, and both teams went at it in ding-dong fashion' according to the *Liverpool Echo.*

Two minutes before half-time and Villa regained the lead, with Crabtree heading past Bob Menham in the Everton goal. What a half the crowd had seen, with five goals and the lead changing hands on three occasions. No wonder they invaded the pitch!

The second half saw more of the same, although at a less frenetic pace as the players tired. Everton, in Percy Young's words, played like 'men possessed' with the best chance falling to Bob Stewart - his free-kick striking the Villa crossbar and bouncing out to safety. On the break Villa still possessed the quality you would expect from the champions, with James Cowan going close twice.

As the underdogs continued to press, the sound of 'Play up Everton' could be heard ringing around the ground. And 'play-up' they most certainly did as they 'swarmed around' Whitehouse in the Villa goal with Bell, Hartley and Milward all wasting good opportunities as the league title-holder's net led a charmed life. The *Liverpool Echo's* report of the final five minutes reflects not only that moment but acts as a perfect summation of the game as a whole:

'The excitement was almost painful, and the Everton forwards, playing with the desperation of despair, showed magnificent form. Their opponents showed themselves fully equal to the occasion and stood up against the hot bombardment.'

As time ticked away Villa broke dangerously and Menham had to punch out a fierce strike by Athersmith, before the referee blew the final whistle. The crowd broke onto the pitch for a second time before Villa received the FA Cup from Lord Roseberry. They were to become the second team to complete the 'Double' and it would be 64 years before it was next achieved. Roseberry – who was a former Prime Minister – was impressed by what he had witnessed and commented: 'The scene of that struggle will live long in the memory.' *Athletic News* agreed with him: 'Those words will be echoed and re-echoed by everyone who saw the contest.'

Everton on the other hand could count themselves unfortunate. Their outstanding performance would surely have been enough to win the Cup against any other opponents – Villa would eventually win the title by 11 points – or in any other year. *Athletic News* confirmed that view: 'On this form they would have beaten any other team than Villa.' They were the first team to lose in a final after scoring twice and, apart from replays, it would be 38 years before it would happen again. But that was certainly no consolation for the players who returned to Lime Street the following day to a small number of fans. *Association Football* was fulsome in its opinion that: 'It was the finest final that has ever been fought.'

POSTSCRIPT:

On a purely statistical basis Fred Geary is one of the most prolific forwards ever to play for the club. A total of 86 goals in 98 matches confirming that he was a magnificent player, one whose 20 goals was the major factor in Everton's inaugural title victory in 1891. After a brief flirtation with Liverpool, he retired and ran the Stanley Arms public house in Westminster Road for 28 years until his death in 1955. Well what has Geary got to do with the 1897 final? Quite a bit actually – for he provided the answer to a 50-year-old mystery surrounding the matchball.

In the early years there was often a dispute about who should keep hold of the ball at the end of the game, with it usually being gathered by the player closest to it at the final whistle. It was not unusual for post-match brawls between players and, on occasions, officials, over possession of the 'leather'. (The rules were changed after the 1933 final between Everton and Manchester City, when match officials and Everton's Albert Geldard, who was holding the ball, clashed as they left the pitch. It was decided thereafter that the referee should be handed the ball and then he would consequently pass it on to the captain of the victorious team).

Shortly before his death in 1949, Will Cuff, who had been chairman of Everton, described the post-match scenes at Crystal Palace in 1897:

'The whole Aston Villa team went into the Everton dressing room after the game demanding the ball be handed back to them. They had seen an Everton player gather the ball and rush off to the Crystal Palace dressing rooms. The Everton players declared that they did not know where the ball was.'

He then described what would now be known as a 'bit of a bundle', as the rivals clashed rather unceremoniously, bearing in mind the occasion. When the atmosphere had pacified a bit, the Villa players searched every part of the dressing room for the ball, including skips and inside clothing, with no luck. But the ball was in the dressing room, as Cuff explained:

'Their search was useless, for an Everton player, realising the difficulty of hiding his treasure, had taken out his penknife as soon as he had got back to the dressing room (interestingly what a player was doing with a knife in a dressing room anyway was never explained by Cuff) and slit the ball. He was proudly going around, among the Villa players, taunting them to: 'Find the ball and you can have it'.'

Where was the ball though? Cuff then elaborated: 'Actually he was wearing it under his football jersey – as a chest protector!'

Although Cuff would not give the name of the knifeman, his identity had already been exposed three years earlier by the journalist Ernest Edwards as Abe Hartley, the Everton forward who played in the match. Hartley died in an accident in Southampton docks in September 1909 – by a twist of fate on the day Everton lost 3-1 to Aston Villa - but before his death he had handed the now reconditioned ball over to his friend Fred Geary, former Everton centre-forward and now keeper of the 'Holy Grail' from the 1897 Cup final.

How long Geary had the ball is unknown, but as he reached his 70s the former player obviously got itchy feet, for when Aston Villa visited Anfield in December 1946, Geary returned the ball to its rightful owners, in a meeting that Edwards had helped to facilitate. Before the match Geary handed the ball over on the pitch to Norman Smith, a Villa director, in a presentation attended by the Liverpool chairman and directors. Curiously there was nobody in an official capacity from Everton.

Even then, according to Cuff, the ball had a rather strange look to it: 'The sight of this ball was worthy of your attention - it was like a seamless ball, the like of which has never been used since, although many a man of genius has tried to invent a ball without seams.'

<hr>

What eventually happened to the matchball?

This is another tale, because nobody knows. Enquiries with Aston Villa staff and historians drew a blank over the whereabouts of the ball used in the final. The mystery still remains.

For the record, a cutting from the *Football Echo* dated 21st December, 1946 provides more detail on how the ball was handed back to the Midlands club. At Liverpool's home game against the Villains, a Villa party are pictured receiving the ball back. The cutting declares: 'Mr Fred Geary, famous Everton centre-forward of the "eighties" hands over to Mr Norman Smith, a director of Aston Villa, the ball with which the Villa club beat Everton 3-2 in the 1897 Cup final. The presentation was made at Anfield today. Also in the picture are Mr W.H. McConnell, Liverpool chairman, and directors J.H. Troop and S.R. Williams.'

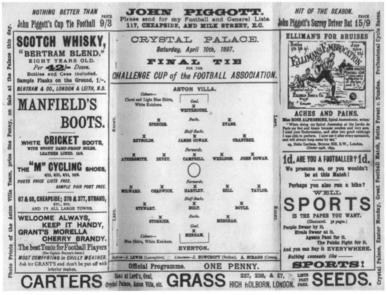

The 1897 FA Cup final programme line-ups

When Fatty sat on Larry

22 stone of trouble
Everton 1-4 Sheffield United
First Division, 30th October, 1897

William 'Fatty' Foulke was a football legend. 'The most talked about player in the world - a leviathan at 22 stone with the agility of a bantam,' according to *The Men Who Made Football* published in 1904. Born William Foulk, he became Foulke during his playing career and then Foulkes after his death of pneumonia in 1916 (like his name, he got bigger and bigger as his life developed, and the keeper was reckoned to be upwards of 26 stone at the turn of the century).

Stories of Foulke abound but many are probably apocryphal. He was once asked about the abuse he received and retorted: 'I don't care what they call me as long as they don't call me late for my lunch,' on account of his prodigious capacity for food. He once was alleged to have arrived early for the team dinner and proceeded to feast off all 11 plates until they were empty. He saved two penalties against Burton Albion and the opposition forward complained: 'Where else could I have placed the kicks. There was nowhere else to aim!'

Although his weight tended to literally overshadow his superb goalkeeping skills, Foulke also had a nasty streak. The game against Sheffield United in 1897 showed both sides of the original football behemoth.

Sheffield came to Goodison at the top of the table, with the home team in their slipstream. United 'had proved to be a wonderful team this season,' according to *Athletic News*. The paper was also unreserved in praising the venue: 'The covered accommodation is something immense and the directors have taken a wise course in attending to the comfort of the gentlemen who regularly place down their sixpence.' Local legend has it that the transport to the match consisted of several carriages, each for four players, but Foulke had one to himself, and it could be seen unsteadily making itself through Walton.

A healthy crowd upwards of 20,000 was present and both teams were given a rousing reception. After surviving some early pressure, the home side went ahead after just four minutes when Williams broke free and set up Larry Bell, who smashed the ball past Foulke. With Everton 'displaying an amount of dash', shortly afterwards Bell broke free and was floored by the Sheffield keeper, but no foul was awarded. As the home side pressed, the giant in goal was called upon several times to repel rampant opponents. But against the run of play Cunningham equalised for United after taking advantage of a mistake by Meehan. A second goal for the leaders arrived shortly after when Almond intercepted a dreadful pass from Johnny Holt. After Priest had broken free on the left shortly before the break, the same player crashed in a volley past McFarlane in the Everton goal.

The second period saw more of the same: constant Everton pressure continually repulsed by the inspired Sheffield custodian, whilst United were dangerous on the break. The *Daily Post* was moved to say that: 'If ever a goalkeeper had the lion's share of the game then Foulke had that on Saturday.' Two saves in particular caught the eye, one was a header from John Cameron that struck him in the face and another was from a dipping shot by Dickie Boyle, which was described as being through 'capital judgement.' (Anyone familiar with press match reports from the 100 or so years ago will recognise 'capital' as a frequently used term to describe excellent play. For some reason the word has disappeared completely over the years.)

Sheffield grabbed a fourth near the end when the right winger Bennett, who had given Storrier on the Everton left the real run-around all day, went on a mazy dribble and blasted home from ten yards out. But shortly before the end came the incident that warrants the inclusion of this game in this book, and is also the basis for the headline at the beginning of the report.

Foulke had a regrettable tendency – for his victims anyway – of using his weight to punish those who were deemed to have offended the big man. If the victim was lucky, this would manifest itself in the target being picked up and swung around. Others had to suffer far worse indignities. One of those poor unfortunates, on this day, was the opposition centre-forward, Larry Bell. The Everton player was the less celebrated sibling of John Bell, a brilliant forward for the club earlier in the decade.

With the scoring complete, contemporary press reports describe a scene at the end of the game in which according to the *Liverpool Echo*, 'Foulkes (sic) in saving fell over Bell, who was injured and had to be carried off the field. Meanwhile the spectators at that end became very noisy, and had to be cautioned as to their future conduct.' Meanwhile the *Mercury* stated: 'It was unfortunate that he (Foulke) should have marred his brilliant performance by an over-use of his weight, for there was an occasion for its use which led to Bell's removal from the field.'

According to *Athletic News*, '...having fisted the ball away, Foulke found Larry Bell in the way and Bell couldn't stand 22 stone and fell like a log and had to be carried off.' Afterwards Foulke 'lifted him up as if he were a child.'

POSTSCRIPT:

What actually happened was that an angry Foulke had purposely decided to sit on Bell just before the final whistle. This was not made public until after Foulke's death. The *Liverpool Echo* carried a piece in the 1920s that clarified the dispute. Bell had, rather unwisely, decided to taunt and tease Foulke after scoring the opener, something the bulky custodian took exception to. 'Fatty' had decided retribution was required, and put all his 22-plus stone on Bell's frame as he used him as a makeshift chair. Bell was seriously injured and needed carrying from the pitch, and was then 'hors de combat' for two weeks. (The same article also points to Foulke trying a similar stunt on a Liverpool player.)

A real heavyweight contest

Jack Hillman was the nearest Everton have had to a Bill Foulke. He weighed in at 17 stone and when the two keepers clashed in the Everton v Sheffield United fixture in 1895, their combined weight came to an astonishing 39 stone, which is four stone more than the largest combined weight for the combatants in any World Heavyweight title clash.

After leaving Goodison Park, Hillman decided to get rid of a few pounds to further his football career - but not those type of pounds. In 1900 the keeper became the first player ever to be found guilty of match fixing. When at Burnley he offered Nottingham Forest players a sum of money (£2 at the start and then £5 at half-time) to take it easy in a crucial relegation match for the Clarets. They refused, Burnley lost 4-0 and were relegated. Word got out and Hillman was summoned before the beak. Although he denied the charges, the keeper was found guilty and was banned for a year.

A hoot at Owlerton

'Drawn game'
Sheffield Wednesday 5-5 Everton
First Division, 12th November, 1904

For the first time in league history four penalties are awarded in one match and, for the only occasion in nearly 5,000 first-team outings, Everton are awarded three spot-kicks in the same game. The Blues also fire five goals past the reigning league champions. But the 5-2 home win over Sheffield Wednesday at Goodison in March 1905 was certainly not the most action-packed game played by Everton in the 1904-05 campaign. In fact, it was not even the most remarkable fixture played between Everton and Wednesday that season.

That honour falls to the stupendous encounter at Hillsborough (or in those days Owlerton Park) four months before. In a list of bizarre Everton matches this would surely feature near the top. Remarkably even the scoreline does not reflect the drama acted out on a cold wintry afternoon in Yorkshire over 100 years ago. The *Daily Express* got it about right: 'It was an afternoon of extraordinary play.'

Everton had enjoyed an inconsistent start to the season, entering the game in fourth place, but were coming off the back of a 5-1 thrashing of Nottingham Forest, courtesy of four goals from Alex Young. Sheffield Wednesday (or The Wednesday as they were officially called until 1929) were going for a hat-trick of league titles and they were handily placed in third before kick-off, level on points with Everton.

The match started in sensational style when Young, continuing his good form, netted on two minutes after he had dispossessed Leyton in the Wednesday defence. The lead lasted just eight minutes, a cross from Simpson being met by Harry Davis and, after his header was partially stopped by Scott in the Everton goal, the England international put the ball over the line at the second time of asking. The home team now moved up a gear and it took a brave challenge from Ashworth to stop Simpson adding a second. Unfortunately for the defender he took a painful blow to the chest and had to leave the field for treatment – he would not be the last player to depart the playing area that day.

Remarkably, in his absence the side flourished, Jimmy Settle netting twice for the visitors midway through the half, the first being a powerful volley direct from a Hardman corner and then he reacted swiftly after the Wednesday keeper Dick Jarvis had fumbled a centre. It was now 3-1 and shortly after Ashworth reappeared from the dressing room and entered the fray to the cheers of the spectators. Ten minutes before the break Everton went 4-1 ahead in front of the disbelieving onlookers, this time Harold Hardman firing home after fine work between Sharp, Settle and Young. 'Their combination was masterly,' according to *Athletic News*. The away side was now toying with their labouring opponents and 'laid siege' to the Wednesday goal; it was no wonder that shortly before the interval Everton went 5-1 ahead. Settle, Young and McDermott all had shots blocked and from Sharp's resulting corner Abbott fired home. So 5-1 to Everton at half-time, with the *Daily Post* describing their first-half performance as one that 'has rarely been exceeded.' Not surprisingly the visitors left the field to a standing ovation.

The second half was even more spellbinding than the opening period, if that were possible. Wednesday moved the dangerous Simpson to inside-left, as they chased the game in the opening period, and were rewarded just after the hour mark when Billy Balmer fouled Simpson in the area. Although Billy Scott saved Stewart's kick, the same player stuck in the rebound, although a suspicion of handball had the Everton players surrounding the referee. To make matters worse there was an injury to Scott, who damaged a collarbone in a collision with Stewart as he netted.

With Scott still struggling and receiving attention, Wednesday peppered the away goal and it was no surprise that Simpson further reduced the arrears, from a Crawshaw cross, midway through the second half - although the *Athletic News* was adamant that a fit keeper would have saved comfortably. Scott was replaced by Walter Abbott soon after, the Birmingham-born full-back who: '...cannot be described as a safe custodian,' according to the *Football Echo* at the time. Everton were now down to ten men for a second time and, with the 20,000 crowd now reaching fever pitch, Stewart slammed one shot against the post before Simpson added his second ten minutes from time after Abbott had saved his initial header. There was now just one goal in it.

Sixty seconds later the match took another unexpected twist. With feelings running high there was a mêlée between Harry Davis and Harold Hardman as they locked horns when challenging for the same ball, the fracas resulting in Davis punching the Everton forward in the face, right in front of the referee. The match official had no choice other than to order the local favourite from the pitch. But despite the loss the Sheffield side still had the upper hand and the Toffees resorted to what was described as 'unsportsmanlike action' that involved regular time-wasting and, on one occasion, after Hardman had strayed offside, Young kicked the ball on purpose into the far-reaches of the crowd. Unusually the referee notified the players that 30 seconds would be added – the half-minute proving crucial as it happens.

With Everton 5-4 up at the end of 90 minutes, the two points were tantalisingly close but this astonishing game had one final act. In a goalmouth scramble at the Everton end, or a 'scrimmage' to use the parlance of the times, the ball dribbled over the goal-line with Bob Ferrier claiming the final touch. The referee immediately blew for full time. This left the crowd (and players) truly shell-shocked from what they had witnessed – ten goals; the home team recovering from a four-goal deficit; Everton down to ten men twice; an injured keeper and a home favourite dismissed for violent conduct. Such a game now would have the press reaching for the superlatives, but in the early 20th century newspapers were far more reserved in describing events. The *Liverpool Echo's* main headline to depict one of the most dramatic domestic matches of all time: 'Match Drawn.'

POSTSCRIPT:

This was a barely credible encounter, one of only 14 league matches to finish 5-5 (Everton also featured in one of the others, against Derby in October 1898). The game even overshadowed the seven-goal thriller at Goodison the following March, when Everton topped the table. Then it was the turn of the home side to start strongly but Makepeace, 'who has a reputation as a safe negotiator of penalty kicks', struck the woodwork with the first penalty of the afternoon. Brittleton put The Wednesday ahead before half-time, only to see to see the home team equalise when Walter Abbott's original spot-kick was saved, and Jack Sharp was on hand to knock in the rebound.

Alex Young made it 3-1 shortly after half-time with two goals within a couple of minutes, before Billy Jones of Wednesday fired wide of Roose in the Everton goal to make it three penalties missed. The referee still had time to award a fourth kick of the day, this time to Everton and Makepeace converted successfully. The veteran Jack Taylor then added a fifth as the title favourites dominated, with Harry Davis netting a consolation for the visitors. What made the match even more noteworthy is that Wednesday had not had a penalty awarded against them for two years, and now they faced three in one match. But, come the end of the season, Everton found themselves bridesmaids yet again, this time finishing a point behind Newcastle. But a game two weeks after the 5-5 match against Wednesday was the main reason why the title was not won – as will be seen shortly.

But the final word on the clash at Owlerton goes to the correspondent from the *Athletic News*. At that time, due to the obvious primitive communications, local match reports were merely a statement of the ebb and flow of the game, and with tight deadlines there was little scope for considered opinion or editorial comment. But *Athletic News* was a weekly paper that was able to take a more in-depth view of the previous Saturday's skirmishes. The match at Owlerton was covered by a journalist known only as 'Tityrus'.

The man with potentially the most embarrassing name in football journalism was understandably gushing in his praise: 'Only with the aid of an airship might I have been able to describe the thrilling end-to-end struggle what was produced at Owlerton on Saturday. But what I can only give is a snap-shot glimpse of the most outstanding game I have ever seen.' It is doubtful whether any of those present would have disagreed with that conclusion.

A circus act at Derby

Everton's other 5-5 draw was a bit of a circus - quite literally. The attendance at Derby County in October 1898 was severely affected by the presence of the Barnum and Bailey Circus next door. As it happened the 7,000 crowd got more than they bargained for in the first 5-5 match in top-flight history. After Larry Bell had put Everton ahead in the opening minutes, the teams swapped goals until the great Steve Bloomer – who as any good Evertonian will tell you, first used the term 'School of Science' to describe the club – scored the final goal from the spot, two minutes from time. In yet another example of 19th century football hooliganism, after a shot from Bloomer was deemed not to have crossed the line: 'Spectators spoke with more force than politeness' to the referee which resulted in the Derby captain John Goodall venturing into the crowd to remonstrate and placate the angry mob.

Ref loses track of time...

...and mistakenly allows a 50-minute second-half at Owlerton in the Sheffield Wednesday v Everton clash of 17th April 1909, with Frank Foxall scoring in what was the 49th minute of the half in a 2-0 win for the home team.

Everton 1909. Back (l to r): Harris, R.Balmer, Scott, Maconnachie, Taylor, Makepeace. Front: Sharp, Coleman, White, Freeman, Young, Turner.

The Everton squad, 1909

Title winners...my Arsenal!
Abandoned game costs Toffees the crown
Woolwich Arsenal 1-3 Everton
Match abandoned: 75 minutes
First Division, 26th November, 1904

Just two weeks after the historic encounter in Sheffield came an equally unforgettable match, for all the wrong reasons in many ways. If the Manor Ground, Oxford was the scene of the greatest renaissance in Everton's history then the unlikely surroundings of the Manor Ground, Plumstead was surely the venue of the biggest injustice – on the park at least - and there's been a few - as Everton were the innocent victims of footballing larceny on a grand scale, although the ramifications were not so apparent at the time.

When abandoned matches are talked about, one game that usually gets a mention is the famous FA Cup tie at Kenilworth Road in 1962 where Manchester City led Luton 6-2 when the match was halted due to a waterlogged pitch after 69 minutes. Denis Law had famously scored all six goals and he, of course, scored in the 'replay' when Luton won 3-1. Not so well known is that there is an Everton connection to those matches as a former Blue, Alec Ashworth, scored both the Hatters' goals in the abandoned game and also netted a brace in their subsequent victory (Ashworth obviously had a liking for scoring two against City, as he had netted twice in the opening five minutes of his Goodison debut against the Manchester side in 1958).

However 58 years earlier there was an even greater wrongdoing perpetrated following an abandoned football game, and this time it was Everton's turn to be on the receiving end. Just two weeks after the 5-5 draw at Sheffield Wednesday, and the point lost in injury time, came a match that was ultimately to have the most profound influence on Everton's quest for the title during the 1904-05 campaign.

At the end of November the Toffees travelled to Plumstead (Arsenal would only move to Highbury in 1913) for the first-ever meeting between the two sides, having lost just once, at home to league leaders Sunderland. The charismatic Welsh international Dick Roose had replaced the injured Billy Scott in the Everton goal whilst Arsenal (or Woolwich Arsenal as they were then known) featured Tim Coleman, a player who was to play a starring role, this time for the Toffees, in an equally controversial game at Chelsea four years later. Also in goal for the Gunners was Jimmy Ashcroft, born in Liverpool and who had actually started his career at Everton in 1897 before moving to Arsenal via Gravesend.

The weather in London was cold and foggy – in fact some fixtures in the capital were postponed – and when the match kicked off in front of a 20,000 gate, the mist meant that it was difficult to discern play on the opposite side of the pitch (the linesmen later confessed that they could not follow the game). The Gunners started the stronger with both Bill Gooing and Coleman going close in the opening moments, and it was hardly a surprise when Linward broke free on the right and crossed to Coleman, who beat Roose with a powerful finish. But the Everton response was immediate. Straight from the kick-off a fine interchange of passes allowed Young – whose place had been in doubt due to lumbago – to burst through unchallenged and fire past Ashcroft.

After half an hour the conditions had worsened, with the fog closing in and the home crowd now quiet as the visitors gained the upper hand. A swift exchange of passes on the right between Jack Sharp and Harold Hardman allowed the latter to beat Ashcroft with a cross-shot into the far post, which meant Everton went into the interval 2-1 up.

During the break the pitch became almost completely blanketed by fog and it was the general opinion that the game should be abandoned, but surprisingly the shadowy figures of the players returned for the second half. The visitors maintained their dominance in this period and within minutes Hardman, Sharp and Taylor spurned good opportunities. But Arsenal were still dangerous on the break, and it took some strong defending from Taylor and Abbott to maintain the Toffees lead.

Twenty minutes from time, with the home team now penned back almost permanently in their penalty area, a corner from the left was knocked in by Young to make it 3-1. But the dense fog made the goal barely visible to anyone present, and consequently before the kick-off the referee called both linesmen together and decided to abandon the match. According to *The Times* their decision was certainly influenced by Jimmy Jackson, the Arsenal captain.

The visitors trudged from the pitch disappointed. In fact, *The Times* would comment that 'the Everton team took the decision unkindly', before adding quite understandably that 'some excuse may be made for them, seeing that barring accidents, or a lightning dash, they were in little or no danger of losing the game.'

So Everton left Arsenal with no reward for their efforts. It was a feeling they would have to get used to over the next 100 years!

POSTSCRIPT:

The abandoning of this game was of crucial significance. The 1904-05 campaign was vigorously contested between Everton, Newcastle and Manchester City and by the time Everton visited Arsenal again in April 1905 for their penultimate match, the title was still at stake. Typically, after dominating the abandoned game, the second encounter was much more evenly contested. Jimmy Settle put the Toffees ahead from the spot but Arsenal equalized with a goal by that fine England international footballer and cricketer, Andy Ducat.

With five minutes left came the ultimate kick in the face. Arsenal broke well and Charlie Satterthwaite put the Gunners 2-1 ahead. To add insult to injury, he was a former Liverpool player. Although the final game at Nottingham Forest was won, it meant that the title was now out of Everton hands. The crucial match was now Newcastle at Middlesbrough. A draw for the away team would be enough for the championship, but the Magpies won and they clinched the title by a point - but Everton would have been champions had fate not so cruelly denied then a win in London six months before. The season was a story of near misses. Everton were also denied in the FA Cup, losing 2-1 in a semi-final replay to Aston Villa.

The only other abandoned game where Everton were leading only to lose the replayed fixture was on 3rd December 1965, during an FA Youth Cup tie at Wrexham. The Blues, who were holders of the trophy, led thanks to a Jimmy Husband goal when the referee called them off due to a waterlogged pitch on 63 minutes. The replayed game saw Everton knocked out thanks to a Wrexham goal – ironically scored in the 63rd minute.

Other Everton abandoned matches

Stockport County (h), 11th January 1913

'Mr Heath was inclined to flout his Arctic Majesty, seeing which the fleecy deity, white with rage, peppered the playing pitch with flaky ammunition.' That was the *Daily Post's* version of the referee's decision to abandon play after 50 minutes with the score at 1-1. Everton won the replayed match 5-1.

Middlesbrough (h), 4th February 1922

Stormy conditions force the referee to abandon the match after 28 minutes of the second half with Everton leading 1-0. The Toffees won 4-1 a month later in the re-run.

Tottenham (a), 17th December 1969

A system breakdown in a nearby electricity sub-station causes the floodlights to fail after 30 minutes with the game goalless. Referee Roger Kirkpatrick waits 47 minutes before abandoning the match in front of a 26,000 crowd. Ironically this match was the second attempt to play the fixture, the original being postponed 18 days earlier due to a poor pitch. The game was finally played in March, when Everton were flying and the Blues won 1-0 on their way to the title.

Bolton (a), 1st January 1979

What was known as the 'winter of discontent', due to the prevailing economic and weather conditions, leaves a very unhappy Peter Reid as a victim. The future Goodison legend breaks his leg, after a collision with Everton's George Wood, in a match that was abandoned at half-time due to the dangerous amounts of snow and ice on the pitch. Allegedly when the Everton players complained to the referee in the first 15 minutes about the conditions, the wonderfully titled Trelford Mills (whose name sounds like a place in Bolton for a start) turned around and said: 'Don't worry, I'm abandoning it at half-time anyway', and in the interim Peter Reid was stretchered off. It was 1-1 at the break – Trevor Ross scoring – and Bolton won 3-1 when it was played again in April with Ross again netting (having already had a goal disallowed - so close to a unique hat-trick).

And one that should have been...

When the press report says that 'for some extraordinary reason at quarter past two the referee decided to start the match when it was absolutely impossible for spectators to see even half the pitch in front of them', it probably means the game should never have taken place. But Everton's game at Wolves in December 1903 did happen, even though most of the action was completely invisible. The *Liverpool Echo* at one stage said: 'Settle (of Everton) was seen shaping towards the home goal but a second later he was lost in the midst of the thick fog.' Such were the conditions that the crowd were allowed at the side of the pitch for a better view.

The paper closed the report by saying: 'The closing stages of one of the most absurd and ridiculous games on record was only seen by the players. A single spectator could not have seen what happened.' The teams apparently drew 2-2.

On the subject of fog at Molineux, Everton keeper Albert Dunlop was the central character in a funny incident there in October 1961. Most of the crowd saw the players leave the pitch until, some minutes after the final whistle, the keeper was seen through the mist in the goalmouth by an ambulance-man, completely oblivious to the end of the game. He was kindly told the match had finished and that his team-mates were probably enjoying a warm bath!

Albert Dunlop (above, left) - Lost in the fog at Molineux

Fireworks at the Bridge

'Everton and Chelsea amazing'
Chelsea 3-3 Everton
First Division, 14th November, 1908

This was a classic, from an explosive start to a finish in almost total darkness, with several controversial flashpoints thrown in along the way. The 40,000 crowd were left breathless with excitement and the *Liverpool Echo's* Ernest Edwards (or Bee as he liked to call himself) was moved to announce that 'the fireworks display should have been fixed for November 14th.'

Everton travelled to the Bridge at the top of the table, their blistering start primarily due to a club-record six consecutive away wins from the beginning of the campaign (a record that still stands). A total of 17 goals had been scored on their travels and just four conceded, highlights including a 5-1 thrashing of Sheffield United and that most satisfying of results – a victory at Anfield, thanks to a goal by George Barlow.

It was Bertie Freeman, though, who was enjoying his own annus mirabilis. The Birmingham-born forward had found the net 15 times in the opening 12 games, and was in the middle of a run that would see him score in ten consecutive league matches. The end of the season would see him accrue a First Division record of 38 goals. The Chelsea star-man was George Hilsdon, a nimble and mobile forward who netted 98 league goals in 150 matches for the London club as well as winning eight England caps.

The beginning of the match was sensational. Hilsdon moved the ball from the kick-off to the Chelsea right, where Brown chested the ball down, beat Makepeace and saw his centre controlled by Hilsdon, who fired past a disbelieving Billy Scott in the Everton goal. It was 1-0 to the hosts, with the strike being timed by the *Liverpool Echo* at ten seconds. It equalled the fastest goal scored against the Toffees in a first-team game.

The visitors were clearly rattled by the unwelcome start and desperate defending was required at times to stop Chelsea adding to their lead. But gradually Everton gained a foothold in the game and Freeman, brimming with confidence, had several optimistic efforts on goal - but these did not impress the watching Bee, who mused that the forward 'did not shoot with wisdom.' The Toffees should then have had a penalty when Sharp was bundled over in the box.

There was then an unusual incident that had the bulk of the crowd celebrating a second successful strike. A shot from Hilsdon looked a certain goal but the ball got wedged, à la Trevor Brooking, between the stanchion and post on the outside of the Everton goal, without passing through the net (Brooking's strike came for England in a World Cup qualifier in Hungary). Inevitably the deflated ball had to be replaced. (A similar event happened notoriously in a Chelsea v Ipswich encounter on the same ground in 1970, when Alan Hudson's shot hit the outside of the side netting, but the referee erroneously awarded a goal, claiming the ball had crossed the line and rebounded out through a hole in the net, even though subsequent checks showed one did not exist.) Just before the interval though Everton got a deserved equalizer when Tim Coleman struck from just outside the box.

The second half was even more pulsating. After Val Harris had struck the Chelsea post, their full-back Jock Cameron headed the ball onto his own bar and, when it fell onto the line, Freeman reacted quickest and slammed his first goal of the afternoon into an empty net. Remarkably the visitors were now 2-1 up. The lead did not last long though as Hilsdon, who had given the normally unflappable Jack Taylor a hard time all afternoon, scored his second, after capitalising on confusion between Balmer and Scott. Almost immediately Everton went back in front, with Freeman scoring his 17th of the season from a Barlow cross, after his first effort had been blocked.

Chelsea then mounted an all-out assault on the Everton goal, and had the ball in the net on no less than three occasions without any effort counting – the first two for offside against Hilsdon and then the third for a foul by two players on Scott in the Everton goal. But on 70 minutes came a decision that rankled for a long period after the game. The match had kicked off at 2.45 in the afternoon and it was now gloomy in the extreme – Bee on his own admission would say it was difficult to see from the press box.

When a cross was played into the Everton penalty area, Billy Scott punched the ball out and when it was returned back towards the net, he skilfully hooked the ball away. But by this time referee Barker, with no appeal by any Chelsea player, had whistled for a penalty on account of handling by Val Harris, even though the player later denied the offence.

Barker was clearly mistaken because of the gathering darkness, as it was clear to everyone that Scott, who was wearing gloves, had handled the ball. *Athletic News* concurred with this view: 'On both occasions Scott clearly punched the ball, his hands were encased in dark woollen gloves.'

What followed was one of the most controversial moments in the early history of the club, as the referee was systematically manhandled by the players ('bumped and pulled about unmercifully' were Bee's carefully chosen words, although he also pointed out the following Monday that they 'hunted the referee in a manner like they looked as though they were going to eat him'). Barker refused to consult his linesmen and when Hilsdon took the resulting penalty, he easily converted the kick for his hat-trick with a furious Scott, under protest, making no effort to save the shot.

The remainder of the match was becalmed by comparison, with both teams having chances, the best of which fell to Hilsdon, but he was denied by a fine save by Scott. The referee blew for full time a short while after to bring to an end 90 minutes of dramatic, entertaining and controversial action. Bee summed up the game with suitable economy: 'Everton and Chelsea amazing.'

POSTSCRIPT:

The *Athletic News* correspondent was equally enamoured with events at the Bridge: 'A remarkable game at Chelsea and calm and mature reflection forces me to the conclusion that the division of six goals was a most equitable result for a game in which we saw much brilliant football. Thrill followed thrill.'

Two other Chelsea classics

November 14th 1931, (h)

The visit of the Londoners in November 1931 was the scene of arguably Dixie Dean's most blistering performance in an Everton jersey: five goals in the opening 32 minutes including the fastest hat-trick of headers in league history, all scored inside the first quarter of an hour.

But in his excellent biography of the great man in 2001, author and broadcaster John Keith recalls Dixie's 'alternative' pre-match preparations for this superhuman feat: 'I had a few pints the night before the game and old

Harry Cooke (the Everton trainer) and I actually slept in the trainer's room at Goodison. We just kipped down in the skips and used the St. John Ambulance blankets to keep warm. Next morning, Harry brought me some coffee and by the time I had my usual sherry and eggs before the game I felt tip top.' One wonders what would have happened if he'd had a good night's sleep!

February 20th 1935, (a)

The match at Stamford Bridge was the scene of one of the most bizarre curios in Everton history. Such was the pattern of play that it was fully 30 minutes from the kick-off before the referee had cause to blow his whistle for a foul. Not only that but two of the goals conceded that day were also out of the drawer marked 'odd.' Joe Mercer's back pass went straight in after Ted Sagar fell over in the mud, and the third in a 3-0 defeat would probably not have happened today. Ted Sagar injured a shoulder and was lying prone on the ground for fully 60 seconds when Barraclough netted for Chelsea. Pity Paolo di Canio was not playing!

Fastest goals against Everton

Grenville Morris	10 secs	Nott'm Forest (a)	23rd December 1905

Enoch West dashed down the right straight from the kick-off, and his shot was pushed out by Billy Scott with Morris firing home the rebound. The time given in the 'Daily Post' was 'inside ten seconds.'

George Hilsdon	10 secs	Chelsea (a)	14th November 1908

Although given as 10 seconds in the 'Liverpool Echo', the 'Athletic News' gives a time of 'inside the first 15 seconds.'

Colin Clarke	11 secs	Bournemouth (h) (FLC)	25th September 1985
Chris Sutton	13 secs	Blackburn (h)	1st April 1995
David Cross	15 secs	Norwich (h) (FLC)	30th October 1973
Jackie Balmer	15 secs	Liverpool (h)	16th February 1938
Derek Kevan	18 secs	West Brom (a)	25th March 1961
Kenny Dalglish	20 secs	Liverpool (h)	21st September 1985

'Uncommon incidents in a grand game'

Forty-two years later there were similar scenes to the one that followed the penalty award at Chelsea in 1908. This time events took place at Goodison during a match against Middlesbrough in August 1950, which was described in the *Liverpool Echo* as having 'many uncommon incidents.' As thunder and lightning flashed around the ground, incessant rain made the pitch completely unplayable due to the pools of water, meaning that even moving the ball several yards became a major trial of strength. There was a curious incident when the conditions became so bad that the referee led the Middlesbrough players off the pitch on their captain's suggestion, whilst the Everton players stayed on as skipper Peter Farrell disagreed.

But the main point of contention arose in the second half when Everton led 2-1. That superb Boro forward Wilf Mannion rose perfectly to head home George Hardwick's cross. The referee immediately pointed to the centre-circle. The home players chased after the official 'like a pack of hounds in full scent' according to the *Liverpool Echo*. Consequently he consulted his linesman and afterwards awarded a free-kick. Strangely the linesman whose comments appeared to change the referee's mind had not flagged for a foul in the first place. It was now the turn of the Boro players to pursue their quarry around the Goodison turf, in scenes that were something akin to the end of the *Benny Hill Show*. However they failed in their mission, and after the match the referee explained he disallowed the goal as Mannion had handled, although most observers remained to be convinced. Incidentally, the Blues won 3-2.

Peter Farrell, doing his best to avoid the attentions of the Toffee lady, refused to go off in 1950

The ultimate game of two halves

0-0 to 5-1 in 13 minutes
Everton 6-1 Blackburn Rovers
First Division, 19th November, 1910

The years prior to the start of World War I are in many ways a sadly ignored golden age of Everton centre-forwards. From the muscle and brawn of Alex 'Sandy' Young to the sublime grace of Bert Freeman and then the extraordinary goal poaching skills of Bobby Parker, the star of the 1914-15 Championship-winning team (the statistics show that Parker monopolized the team's goalscoring in a manner that is unmatched by any other player in the club's history, including Dixie Dean).

The 1910-11 season was typical of that period, the team being more than a match for most but falling short when it really mattered. By the time Blackburn visited Goodison in November 1910, the normally prolific forward line had misfired in the opening 12 matches, netting just 12 goals with the Toffees having won six and lost five games. Freeman had been injured against Arsenal at the beginning of the month and would only play one more match for the club. It was also to be Young's last season with Parker's arrival two years off.

Everton gave a debut to Jim Meunier at left-back due to an injury to Bob Balmer, whilst Rovers featured our old friend Jimmy Ashcroft, the Arsenal keeper in the notorious abandoned match at Highbury in 1904. Everton enjoyed the best of the early exchanges with Ashcroft saving well from a header by Bob Young (no relation to Alex) and Harry Makepeace. The home side stepped up the pressure before the break, with Alex Young firing wide when well placed. The crowd met the half-time whistle with indifference though as the game had clearly not matched expectations. They would more than be satisfied in the second half as it transpired.

The *Athletic News* reporter described what happened then in typical grandiose terms: 'No greater contrast can be imagined than that which was generated by the play in the first and second halves, goal followed goal with a regularity I have never seen before.' Within three minutes of the re-start

Everton broke on the right, but the cross was too deep and ended up at the feet of George Barlow on the opposite side of the pitch. His cross was perfectly placed for Alex Young, who did not have to break stride and drove the ball high into the net from inside the six-yard box. The joy of the home side was short-lived though as Rovers came back with Billy Garbutt firing home past Scott after finding space in the Blues box on 50 minutes.

It was at that point that the game went out of control. Four minutes after the equalizer Alex Young ran strongly through Rovers' defence and powered a venomous shot from 25 yards straight past Ashcroft for his second of the afternoon. Two minutes after it was George Beare's turn to influence proceedings, 'racing along like a warhorse,' according to the *Liverpool Echo*, he put Everton 3-1 up after Rovers' Tommy Suttie – who should have played sweeper with a name like that - failed to clear a cross. With Rovers now in complete disarray, a minute later it was Irish international Bill Lacey – the only player in the 20th century to win international caps with both Everton and Liverpool – who scored Everton's fourth, with a shot from inside the box from Barlow's cross. Three minutes later and it was another goal, this time Beare bravely scoring his second. From 0-0 to 5-1 in 13 minutes! The *Liverpool Echo* was typically colourful in the portrayal of this spree: '…Everton slashed through the Blackburn ranks as would a troop of cavalry through a crowd of rebellious yokels', whilst the *Athletic News* proclaimed: 'The pent-up forces in the Everton ranks broke forward with a hurricane rush.'

The crowd had to wait fully ten minutes for the final goal when, having seen the Toffees' Billy Scott save a penalty from Bill 'Tinker' Davies, Alex Young completed his hat-trick after a mesmeric individual run and shot. The last 20 minutes were an anti-climax, the home side being happy to retain possession whilst Rovers were happy to engage in a damage limitation exercise. At full time the home team left the pitch to roars of acclaim from the home crowd, who had just witnessed one of the greatest scoring blitzes in Everton history.

POSTSCRIPT:

After a 6-1 thrashing, the last thing Blackburn wanted was another meeting, but they had to play Everton again – two days later! This time in the Lancashire Cup at Ewood Park and, typically, the game was the complete opposite of the league meeting, with this time it being Rovers' turn to win 6-1, a victory that included three goals in a five-minute spell.

McIntyre runs riot

Twelve years after this flurry of goals, Everton were on the receiving end of the most sustained burst of scoring by a single player in English football history, with the opponents again being the Lancashire side. After taking the lead through a George Harrison penalty at Ewood Park in September 1922, they were pegged back when Rovers equalised just before the break. Then between the 55th and 59th minute the following took place:

55 mins: John McIntyre puts Rovers 2-1 up with a fine shot from a Hodkinson centre.
57 mins: McIntyre fires past Tom Fern from a Bond pass.
58 mins: Another scramble in the box and McIntyre completes his hat-trick.
59 mins: With the crowd in a state of frenzy, McIntyre shoots past a bewildered Fern after an exchange of passes with Bond.

The Rovers forward had netted four times in five minutes, the fastest time in which a player has recorded a quartet of goals in England. Rovers eventually won the game 5-1. On the same day Liverpool scored five goals in 15 minutes at Anfield.

Everton conceded three goals in the space of 125 seconds at Burnley on 16th March 1974, the goals being scored by Colin Waldron (76 mins, 20 secs), Geoff Nulty (77 mins, 10 secs) and the final goal in a 3-1 defeat was netted by Leighton James after 78 minutes, 25 seconds.

Jack Taylor (left) and Alex 'Sandy' Young shake hands on their FA Cup success in 1906

The Magnificent Seven
Cup tie kicks off
Everton 3-0 Barnsley
FA Cup 1st round, 9th January, 1915

The 1914-15 season was one of the most controversial in league history. The campaign took place against the backdrop of the First World War and some observers, understandably, were uncomfortable with the game being played competitively whilst hundreds of thousands were losing their lives a short hop away across the Channel. Sense prevailed when league football was suspended at the end of the season.

Everton had just been crowned champions for the second time with a total of just 46 points from 38 games - the ravages of war had deprived several clubs of players and as a result the campaign was more closely fought than usual. Under the three-points-for-a-win rule, the champions' total equates to 65 points, which would have been enough for only fifth place in 2005-06.

For much of the season the elusive Double seemed to be on, as the Toffees reached the semi-finals of the FA Cup, but a poor performance at Villa Park against Chelsea ended those dreams.

But the FA Cup run featured one of the most remarkable matches ever played at Goodison, when Second Division Barnsley visited in the first (now the third) round. The Toffees were on a good run of form going into the match, having taken 14 out of a possible 18 points in their previous nine league matches. There was also a scent of revenge in the air, as the Tykes had turned over Everton in a bad-tempered semi-final in 1910, when the career of Jack Taylor was ended after he had been struck in the throat. The Blues lost 3-0 that day but they were firm favourites to triumph at home on this occasion.

From the start of the game it was clear that Barnsley were intent on spoiling the game with some robust tactics. The first bad foul was committed by Barnsley's Fred Barson on George Harrison, which warranted a booking by the referee, Mr T.B. Sephton. Although the *Liverpool Echo* did report that: 'Everton were determined to play Barnsley at their own game with Galt delivering some lusty charges.' The home side had most of the early pressure with Harrison going close on two occasions and Clennell's shot was headed out from under the bar by a Barnsley defender. From the resulting corner, Harrison put the ball into the middle of the area and Galt moved quickly to knock the loose ball in. But a few minutes later there was the first major flashpoint of the tie. A clash between Barson and Harrison saw the Barnsley player lying injured behind his own goal, although it was not clear to most observers what had happened. When he returned to his feet the referee ordered both players off the pitch. *Athletic News* then takes up the tale:

'When he (Barson) recovered, both he and Harrison marched from the Bullens Road side of the ground towards the dressing room. Barson and Harrison dramatically shook hands before bidding farewell to the crowd.'

The referee at half-time clarified his position: Barson had been dismissed for taking the feet away from underneath Harrison whilst Harrison's retaliation – he kicked Barson whilst the Barnsley player was on the floor – was also enough to warrant a dismissal.

Six minutes later Bobby Parker added a second for the home team, hooking the ball past Cooper in the Barnsley goal (Parker would score 40 goals for Everton that season, including 38 alone in the league). Both Makepeace and Chedgzoy then missed opportunities to secure victory for the home side before the break. Barnsley showed greater imagination in the second half, and for the first time showed a genuine threat to the Everton goal. Lees mis-kicked completely when he had only Tom Fern in the Everton goal to beat and then Maconnachie kicked a shot from Tufnell off the line. But this was all the Tykes had to offer in what was a poor performance, 'a disorganised eleven' was the *Athletic News* viewpoint.

Thirteen minutes into the second half came another sensational incident - Bobby Parker charged Cooper in the Barnsley goal, and then proceeded to kick his opponent. The referee saw no other option than to send the prolific forward off, whilst the goalkeeper frantically tried to persuade the referee to keep Parker on the pitch. To give an idea to how much of a shock this was, prior to the match Everton had had only five players sent off in their entire history, so two in the same match was regarded as sensational.

But *Athletic News* was candid in the criticism of the man in the middle: 'The referee sending players off in that manner meant that his decisions in both cases created undisguised astonishment in the minds of the majority of onlookers', before adding that 'the crowd grew sarcastic, and real interest in the game vanished.' The *Liverpool Echo* took the opposite view, praising the referee for his capable handling of events: 'Mr Sephton controlled the game well, he was very strict and exceedingly keen, and it was just as well he was so, otherwise many more objectionable incidents might have happened.' Several of the crowd vented their anger by throwing fruit onto the pitch, although the *Liverpool Echo's* view was that the match was 'not dirty in the sense accepted by the football world, but was exceedingly toughly fought.'

Within a minute Everton, now down to nine men, made it 3-0, this time Jimmy Galt scoring from just outside the penalty area from a direct free-kick. Whilst all this was going on Jimmy Clennell was really struggling, having been unwell prior to the game. Worryingly, the Everton forward then fainted in full view of the 19,000 crowd and was taken from the pitch. This meant the home side were now down to just eight men, with the forward line of five players being reduced to just two.

Astonishingly the team was down to just SEVEN men shortly after, when Tom Fleetwood was forced to retire through an injury. At this point in the game there were just 17 out of the original 22 players on the pitch, but thankfully due to their three-goal lead, Everton were able to hang on to secure a famous victory.

POSTSCRIPT:

At the end of this memorable match there was no doubt who was regarded as the pantomime villain. The referee left the pitch under a cloak supplied by Will Cuff, the club chairman, and was surrounded by the players for protection as an angry throng bayed for blood. Goodness knows what would have happened if Everton had actually lost.

After the match the crowd had gathered around the players' room and had to be moved on by police and officials to Spellow Lane, whilst the referee and a linesman left by taxi through a back entrance.

During the following week it also transpired that goalkeeper Willie Cooper of Barnsley had immediately written to the FA to try and get Parker's dismissal scrubbed from the records – to no avail, as he would later serve a one-match suspension. One local writer in the *Liverpool Echo* sarcastically derided the referee's performance the following weekend: 'The referee apparently thought the place was too crowded, so he sent three men off to create a bit of breathing space.'

Gloves off at Goodison

Friendly with a difference
Everton XI 3-1 Boxers XI
Friendly, 28th April, 1915

When Jack Sharp was at Everton he set up his famous sports' shop in Whitechapel, and it was his sporting connections that in 1915 enabled him to set up a friendly match to support the Sailors and Soldiers Association, after the start of World War I. But this was no ordinary friendly - the former Blue thought it would be a good idea to organise a game between Everton's 1906 FA Cup-winning team and a side consisting of boxers. The latter side consisted of some of the biggest names from the sport in Britain and as it turned out they were no mugs at football (but nobody would have told them otherwise, probably).

Eight of the historic 1906 line-up were available with only Alex Young, Harry Bolton and Jack Crelley absent. Their places were taken by the former Liverpool striker Jack Parkinson (who had been a thorn in the side of the Blue half of Merseyside in the first half of the century) and 1890s legends Edgar Chadwick and John Bell respectively.

The star-turn in the boxers' line up was Bombardier Billy Wells, reigning British Heavyweight champion and one of the best fighters of the first quarter of the 20th century. (Wells has another claim to fame, in that he was the man striking the gong at the start of films made by the Rank organisation.)

Also in the line-up was Bandsman Dick Rice, who had three contests against Wells for the British title, the first of which had been a loss on points over 20 rounds at Liverpool Stadium 12 months previously. The rest were an eclectic mix of pugilists including Tancy Lee, who would later fight the legendary Jimmy Wilde for the British flyweight title. In goal was heavyweight Gordon Sims, who was rumoured to have played football for a Southern League club. The referee was club captain Jimmy Galt and the former England Test cricketer Johnny Tyldesley was a linesman. Lord Derby took the kick-off.

Tancy Lee went close early on and it was soon clear that the boxers' superior fitness would clearly be advantageous. But midway through the first period Settle played a fine through ball to Parkinson, who scored easily. But before the interval Wells (who surprisingly was not at centre-forward, taking the inside–right position) equalised 'amid much enthusiasm,' according to the *Daily Post*.

At half-time John Bell exchanged places with Parkinson at centre-forward and the great man showed he had lost none of his potency in front of goal when he put the footballers 2-1 up. Near the end a fine run and cross by Sharp himself set up Chadwick (who was now 45) to nod past Sims.

Although mischievously wishing for what would have been an interesting punch-up, following a crude tackle perhaps, the crowd stood to applaud all the combatants at the end, in a match that was played in a good spirit. The 12,000 gate was good for the times (Everton had just won the title and the draining effects of the First World War had resulted in an average of 19,000) and the funds raised were invaluable.

Jack Sharp (left) and Bombardier Billy Wells, key players in the 1915 friendly encounter

Play it again, Sam

Corner-kick controversy
Everton 2-3 Arsenal
First Division, 15th November, 1924

There is no doubt that the single most debated action carried out by any Everton player in a first-team match was the one undertaken by winger Sam Chedgzoy at Goodison Park in the 1924-25 season. Such was the furore that it led directly to a change in the rules of the game, but there is a lot more to this story than has generally been written about in the past.

The background to what was a rather complex controversy lay in the change to the rules of the game, as agreed by the International Board, to allow for goals scored direct from a corner-kick. This was relevant to what was then Law 10, which prior to the 1924-25 season stated that a 'corner-kick' should be subject to the same treatment as a 'free-kick', and the kicker could not play the ball from a free-kick or corner-kick a second time 'until it had been played by another player.'

However, in changing the law for the start of the 1924-25 season to allow for a goal scored direct from a corner, any reference to the phrase 'corner-kick' was erroneously removed from Law 10 and the new Law 11 said: 'A goal may be scored from a corner-kick, or from a free-kick.' As there was no other definition of a corner-kick within the laws of the game, in essence it meant that a corner could be played more than once before another player touched it, as there was nothing within the laws to state otherwise.

The irony was that the idea, which originated from the Scottish FA, was rejected by their English counterparts. Only a late change in the constitution of the Board enabled the motion to be passed. What also complicated matters was that the Referees' Guide or 'Chart' was left unchanged for the new season, so officials were effectively operating under the old rules.

The man popularly credited with highlighting the anomaly was Ernest Edwards, our old friend 'Bee', sports editor of the *Liverpool Echo*. Bee brought the omission to the attention of readers in late October 1924 and his revelation certainly caused him to fall foul of the Liverpool Referees'

Society, and a deputation from that group verbally challenged the reporter outside the newspaper's offices! The Society made it clear that they would not allow a kicker to touch the ball twice from a corner in any matches in the city. Although Bee claimed that he alone had spotted the anomaly, this was not technically true. For instance *The Times* reported that 'it was an oversight noticed since the start of the season, but nobody has taken advantage of it.'

Edwards surmised that it would be possible for a player to dribble the ball from a corner and was prepared to offer £2 for someone from Everton or Liverpool to test this out in a match – although within the law, it would certainly be regarded as not being within the spirit of the game. Now, although it was Everton's Sam Chedgzoy who eventually took up the offer, it is not so well known that Edwards first made an approach to Donald McKinlay of Liverpool, who at first agreed and then reneged on the deal in case he was accused of poor sportsmanship and bringing his club into disrepute.

The date was set between Edwards and Chedgzoy as 15th November 1924, when Everton would be entertaining Arsenal at Goodison. Interviewed by the *Liverpool Echo* many years later, chairman Will Cuff outlined the 'contract' between the two men, one that, had it existed today, would surely have had major repercussions for all concerned. Cuff said:

'Bee then offered the fee (£2) to Chedgzoy with but one proviso: 'Get that corner in the first 20 minutes if possible as I want to feed my newspaper clients around the country with the full story, and if it arrives after then the wires I send will not reach London, Manchester, Preston, aye, every big town, in time for publication'.'

On the day of the game Everton were in 17th place after 14 matches, with only three matches won and 13 goals scored. The Gunners, meanwhile, were in their pre-Herbert Chapman phase and were not the force they would become in later years. The Toffees line-up was not a bad one to be fair, featuring Alec Troup, that cultured defender Hunter Hart and up front Wilf Chadwick, who had been the country's leading scorer the previous season. The Gunners featured Jock Rutherford, a winger who had just turned 40 and who had been playing professionally for over 20 years. He would actually have a part to play in the events. Both keepers were untried: Bob Jones in the Everton goal was making his home debut whilst it was the first Arsenal appearance for Dan Lewis at the other end.

Chedgzoy had a couple of attempts on the day to score a goal using the 'new rule.' As early as the first minute he was as good as his word to Edwards, forcing a corner at the Park End but failing to score. Not privy to the agreement between the two parties, 'the spectators were getting waxier and yelled instruction what he should do with the ball' according to Cuff, who then described the extraordinary lengths the Everton winger was going to meet Edwards' demand:

'Chedgzoy was hanging onto the ball to try to force an early corner-kick. It was the funniest interlude for years. The crowd shouted to Chedgzoy: 'Centre, centre' but he wanted a full-back to home near enough to force the ball onto his leg for a corner.'

As Everton continued to pressurise the Gunners, the England international forced another corner and was presented with another opportunity to 'test' the rule. As arranged, he dribbled in and glanced up at the referee to see if he was objecting, but the man in the middle had obviously read the new rules and did not object, allowing Chedgzoy to run in and drive in a shot, which unsuccessfully did not find the target.

Edwards' match report states: 'The crowd looked on with astonishment at such a procedure, but they were not exactly ignorant of the move, because for a fortnight now this rule and its reading has been the subject of a big debate in Bee's Notebook (his weekly column in the *Football Echo*).'

The rest of the match itself could only have been an anti-climax, although it did have its moments, and later on in the second half, Rutherford of Arsenal tried to copy Chedgzoy from the same corner flag. The Arsenal winger actually dribbled further than his Everton counterpart, but again just failed to score.

Aside from the efforts of the respective wingers, the rest of the game saw Arsenal go in front just before half-time when Jimmy Ramsay struck a tremendous shot from long range that hit the crossbar, bounced down and then went in off the young Everton keeper. Bobby Irvine equalised for the Toffees just after the break, after a fine dribble and shot and then Frank Hargreaves put Everton ahead after Lewis in the Arsenal goal had failed to handle a Chedgzoy centre. But just after the hour the dangerous Andrew Young, the visiting centre-forward, hammered a glorious drive past Jones to make it two goals apiece.

Then, after Rutherford had tried to copy Chedgzoy, Arsenal netted the winner near the end when a goalmouth scramble resulted in Ramsay bundling the ball over the line. Ironically the goal originated from a corner taken in the orthodox method by the Arsenal winger. The Gunners then held on for a well-merited victory.

POSTSCRIPT:

The national newspapers did cover the controversy. The *Manchester Guardian* mentioned that 'an unusual feature of the game was the method of taking corners, began by Everton and copied by Arsenal.' The *Daily Mail,* under the headline 'Curious incident at Goodison Park', covered the legislative background whilst the *Daily Telegraph* did not mention it at all in its report!

But like the Spurs FA Cup match in 1937, which is covered later, a bit of football mythology has grown up around this incident over the years, which has succeeded only in exaggerating the events that happened on the pitch. Most history books claim the incident took place at White Hart Lane and that Chedgzoy dribbled the ball across the goal line and passed the ball into the empty net, in front of stunned players and officials. (Although Chedgzoy did score at White Hart Lane in 1924, it was actually in April of that year, before the law had been changed, and he scored with a fine cross-shot in a 5-2 victory.)

The tale normally goes that at half-time the winger showed everyone the rulebook to show he was right, usually pointing out that the referee now allowed 'the goal', having previously disallowed it. Actually what did happen, which was not made public until several years after, was that Edwards was allowed access to the dressing room at half-time by Will Cuff, in order to visit Chedgzoy, where he paid him the £2 and remarked: 'Thanks for the fun', before being asked to leave by an Everton official. At no point did Chedgzoy show any rulebook to a club or match official.

The point Edwards was trying to make was that the law as it stood was full of holes and could be exploited, and he just wanted someone to prove that in a high-profile match (as well as servicing his own ego it should be added). Edwards was of the view that the law should remain unchanged, as by allowing dribbling from corner-kicks it added an extra dimension to play and also increased the uncertainty in the opposition defences.

There was one other intriguing aspect to the issue, which has never been mentioned previously. Research by the author has established that when

Preston played Nottingham Forest on the very same day at Deepdale, George Harrison of the home side took a corner in the same manner as Chedgzoy, but was erroneously penalised by the referee, who awarded a free-kick against him. Harrison was a former Everton team-mate of Chedgzoy and, as it is probably too much of a coincidence that both should do it independently, the only conclusion is that Harrison had been tipped off by the Everton winger. Of interest as well, is that the author has discovered that the Everton man was not the first to try it. The same stunt had been pulled by a player for the British Army earlier in the season, who not only dribbled but succeeded in scoring from the shot, with the goal being allowed.

The rules would be changed to stop such an action happening again, but not before this was printed in the *Liverpool Echo*, which summarised the confusion resulting from Chedgzoy's actions:

Little Jack Horner
Taking a corner
Pulled out his rule book quick
And found he could dribble
Right into the middle
Instead of the orthodox kick

So little Jack Horner
Dribbled his corner
Thinking he'd not get far
But the referee blew not
Jack got in shot
And now we don't know where we are

And Little Jack Horner
All through this darned corner
Has got football fans all awry
With all their fine schooling
They can't read the ruling
Oh! Why did you do it, Chedgzoy?

Sam Chedgzoy's career after leaving Everton in 1926 is equally intriguing. Having been on vacation to Canada in 1922, he was tempted over to North America where he played for four seasons for the New Bedford Whalers in the American Soccer League. In 1930 he went to Canada to coach the Montreal Carsteel side in the Canadian National Soccer League. He continued playing and appeared in the National Soccer League final in 1939 at the age of 49, where Carsteel won the second of their three final victories under his leadership. Chedgzoy then worked for the Canada Car and Foundry Company until his death in 1967. His son was also on Everton's books as a junior.

Penalty rule changed

This is not the only episode in an Everton game that has resulted in a change to the football rulebook. The first occurred just three years before, in April 1921, when an incident occurred in the away game at Oldham that indirectly necessitated an amendment in the rule appertaining to penalty kicks. Oldham were awarded a spot-kick and David Wilson easily scored past Tom Fern, but the referee had noticed that the keeper had advanced from his line and ordered the kick to be retaken, even though the original was successful. Guess what happened next? Wilson's retaken kick was saved by Fern, and Everton won 1-0. The law was subsequently changed to its current form - a goal stands if a penalty is successfully converted regardless of whether the keeper has committed an offence.

'The Carr Plan'

The above was a headline on the back page of the *Liverpool Echo* on Monday 5th October, 1970, the story concerning the Employment Minister, Robert Carr. But at Highfield Road two days earlier there was an alternate 'Carr Plan', this time involving the Coventry City midfielder Willie Carr and the former Everton player Ernie Hunt. When a free-kick was awarded just outside the box towards the end of the game, Carr stood over the ball, gripped it with both heels, leapt into the air to flick it behind him and then dived out of the way as Hunt executed a beautiful first-time volley that flew past Rankin in the Everton goal.

Match of the Day captured the moment for posterity and the strike was voted deservedly as 'Goal of the Season'. But in what was a delicious irony, the move was deemed illegal and was 'banned' by the authorities. The reason? Carr, by holding the ball between two feet, was deemed to have touched the ball twice before another player touched it. Sounds familiar?

Incidentally Ernie Hunt gave his version of events to *The Evertonian* in 2005:

"I went over to Willie and on the tape you can see me gesturing to him as if to say: 'Flick it up, flick it up.' Everton were faffing about setting the wall up and everything and Willie flicked it up. Dave Clements came across trying to get in on it but I managed to hit it and catch it just right. It went in the top corner and that was that.

"The atmosphere afterwards was really strange. Everyone was cheering and then it all stopped before you could hear people all chattering away to themselves.

"There was a buzz around the ground with people obviously saying: 'Goodness me, I've never seen that before!'

"Roger Kenyon said to me: 'I was the one that ducked otherwise you wouldn't have scored!' and goalkeeper Andy Rankin told me I had a lot to thank him for!"

Sam Chedgzoy (left) and Ernie Hunt (above) - 20th century innovators

Match of a century

A travesty of a result
Fulham 1-0 Everton
FA Cup third-round replay, 14th January, 1926

The 1920s were not exactly a glorious period in the usually proud association of Everton with the FA Cup. Aside from a quarter-final berth in 1921, there were ignominious defeats at home to Crystal Palace (6-0 - Everton's record FA Cup defeat) and to Brighton (5-2 away). As the omnipresent 'Bee' said in the *Liverpool Echo* at the time: 'For some years now they have been tainted with shyness in Cup-ties.'

On face value, a 1-0 defeat at Craven Cottage to Second Division Fulham in 1926 fits perfectly into this pattern of underachievement. But nothing could be further from the truth. It was one of the most one-sided matches in the club's history, fit to rank with the unrewarded mauling of Grimsby Town at Goodison in 1984, or the 1-1 draw against Panathanaikos in the European Cup 13 years before that freak defeat.

The first game at Goodison was the first-ever meeting between the teams, and was a non-descript affair in front of a crowd of 46,000 where the man-of-the-match was the young Fulham keeper, Ernie Beecham, who kept the home side at bay with a confident display. But it did see the first of the club-record 28 goals scored by Dixie Dean for the Toffees in the competition.

The replay was in London on the following Thursday, and it was undoubtedly not the greatest day in the career of the legendary No 9. The match was played in thick snow and, in what was probably a unique occurrence in an Everton match, a team of workmen surrounded the pitch throughout the 90 minutes, brushing the snow away to keep the touchlines visible. The victor was to be rewarded with a home tie against Liverpool, so the incentive was certainly there for the Toffees.

It was quickly apparent that a match against their local rivals was certainly motivating the visitors. They belied their poor form in the league, with the Second Division side chasing shadows from the start as the Toffees moved the ball swiftly around the snow-laden pitch. Such was the Blues' dominance that the normally withdrawn half-back line of Bain, Virr and Peacock played deep inside the Fulham half. After 20 minutes Sam Chedgzoy struck a powerful drive that hit the right-hand post with Beecham well beaten - it would be the first of four occasions that the woodwork would save the Cottagers.

After the Fulham full-back Dyer had cleared a Dean effort off the line, the Everton centre-forward had the perfect chance to score as Beecham spilled a cross, but the youngster struck the crossbar from a couple of yards out. Although the referee mysteriously blew for offside, it was typical of the afternoon. Just before the break the post was struck for the second time - again Dean being the unfortunate victim.

At this stage the home side had gone 1-0 up and, in keeping with the pattern of the clash, it was the Blues who had self-destructed. After half-an-hour which, in Bee's words, Everton had tried 'stabbing drives, free-kicks, drives, hooks, lobs and headers' at the home goal, David Bain mis-kicked in the visitors' penalty area and when keeper Harry Hardy failed to grab the loose ball, Bert White slipped the ball into the empty net. It was the only time in the 180 minutes that Fulham had posed any sort of threat.

The second half saw more of the same. Everton laid siege to the home goal but the harder they tried, the more outrageous became both Beecham's, and his team's luck. The *Daily Mail's* observation that 'fortune proved a good 12th man for the home team' was certainly true. If the keeper – described in the newspaper as being 'here, there and everywhere' - did not stop the Everton forwards then the woodwork came to the rescue, with John O'Donnell and Dean – again – both striking the post. Dyer also saved his keeper by kicking off the line for the second time.

The Blues' final chance came in the dying minutes when Troup struck the ball well from 20 yards only to see the young keeper catch the ball brilliantly at the foot of the right-hand post. That was it. The Blues had given everything but not for the first time, good fortune had deserted them. Beecham was carried shoulder-high by Fulham supporters at the end of the game. Everton went off to cheers from their 12 (!) supporters. Bee, as ever, summed it all up perfectly: 'This was the match of a century, and there won't be another one for at least another century.'

POSTSCRIPT:

If it's any consolation, Fulham beat Liverpool 3-1 in the next round. The tie firmly established the London side as a bogey side for the Blues in the FA Cup, a mantle they have unfortunately kept ever since. Twenty-two years later the sides reunited in a fifth-round tie at Craven Cottage, with Fulham still plying their trade in Division Two. A 1-1 draw was followed by a 1-0 win for the London side – who also missed a penalty - at Goodison in front of 71,000. In 1975 a fifth-round tie also caused heartbreak, this time a 2-1 defeat would have been different if Clive Thomas – yes, him again - had not disallowed a Mick Lyons effort. A fourth-round tie in 2004 also ended predictably with a Fulham win in a replay.

Cup hopes deflated

Twelve months later and it was more heartbreak from an unexpected source, this time via the match ball. The fourth-round tie against Hull had gone to a third game at Villa Park, and with the match locked at 2-2 near the end of extra time came an extremely odd goal. A Hull corner was volleyed by George Martin – whose impressive performances would result in a transfer to Goodison shortly after – but when he struck the ball it burst almost instantly before sailing into the net. The referee, somewhat controversially, allowed the goal, even though the rulebook stated that a burst ball is a 'dead' ball and play should stop. Despite protests, the goal stood and Everton went out of the competition in the most unusual circumstances imaginable.

24 corners and still lost

The record number of corners won by Everton in a single game is 27 – in the 6-2 win over Keflavik in the European Cup in 1970. In February 1954 the Toffees, then in Division Two, travelled to Hillsborough, where they went out of the FA Cup in front of a crowd of 65,000. Having played supremely well they had kept the game at 1-1 until Wednesday scored twice in the final ten minutes. The *Evening Express* at the time used to run what was called the 'Football Accountant' – a statistical analysis of the featured match. The data on the tie read as follows (see overleaf):

	Everton	Sheffield Wednesday
Goals	1	3
Mins in opponents half	32	24
Corners	24	7
Goal-kicks	10	23
Free-kicks	15	8
Offside	2	5
Shots at goal	8	9

The Toffees had most of the territorial advantage and forced 24 corners, with the amount of goal-kicks indicating how much of the play was in their opponent's box – and they still got beat. In November 1995 during a Premiership game against Wednesday, they won 25 corners but could only finish with a 2-2 draw.

Sewell's flick-on is converted by Shaw (unseen) for Wednesday's first in the 1954 clash at Hillsbrough. According to the original caption, Donovan (No 2) 'played the game of his life'

Wainwright's shot beats McIntosh, but also the post as the Blues go close to taking a 2-1 lead - the same player had earlier hit the bar with another effort

Foxes fight back

Three-goal lead lost
Everton 3-4 Leicester City
First Division, 18th September, 1926

The 1926-27 campaign was one of the most miserable in the club's history, the Blues finishing just one place above relegation in 20th place - the lowest ever at that point. A total of 90 goals were conceded. A promising forward called Dean was absent for the first 13 matches following his serious motorcycle accident, of which only one was won - against Liverpool of all people. But his return to the side saw him finish with 21 goals in just 27 matches to effectively keep the team in the top flight.

One match in that dreadful start was a home game against Leicester City in September, when the Toffees were still looking for their first league goal at Goodison. Dean was still absent at that point in time and his replacement was David Bain, nominally a central defender whose record of 32 appearances and no goals for the club was not exactly a pre-requisite for filling the great man's boots. Leicester on the other hand were well served in the attacking department, featuring Arthur Chandler at centre-forward – a player who netted 259 league goals for the Foxes. Strangely Chandler never scored a penalty for Leicester in his entire career, his only spot-kick being saved by Howard Baker at Chelsea in 1924, and coincidentally it was Baker who was the Everton keeper for this match.

The match was just five minutes old when Irvine broke through in the inside-right channel and weighted a perfect through ball for Bain to open the club's account at Goodison for the season past Ken Campbell in the Leicester goal. (Campbell, it should be noted, was also the Liverpool keeper when Everton recorded their biggest-ever derby win at Anfield, 5-0 in 1914. The veteran Scot had obviously given out the wrong message by wearing a blue shirt at the start of that match, and had to replace it after five minutes.)

The goal instilled some confidence into the home side's play, and they knocked the ball about the pitch with gusto. Campbell was in fine form: 'A difficult proposition for any forward as the people of Liverpool should know,' according to the *Liverpool Echo*. Today's highlights included a full-length save from Irvine, the Scot pushing the ball around the post. But the keeper was at fault on 33 minutes when he arrived late for a Troup corner-kick and watched helpless as Irvine nodded the ball into an unguarded net. After a few close shaves it was 3-0 five minutes later, Irvine crashing home his second of the game from just inside the box. So 3-0 at half-time – surely the home side were odds-on for their first win of the campaign, weren't they?

After the break the Blues were facing a stiff breeze and also a glaring sun, which had unexpectedly made an appearance during the break. As a result the second half was a slightly different proposition to the opening period. On 52 minutes a cross from Billy Bell on the left was met perfectly by Chandler, who volleyed the ball past the stranded Baker in the Everton goal. Just two minutes later the Foxes were really back in the game when Chandler nipped in to poach a second from a loose ball in the Blues penalty area. Everton continued to break well but found Campbell in brilliant form – pushing away powerful strikes from Bain and then Troup.

But at the other end it was Leicester who were enjoying the best of the play with Ernie Hine, a clever inside-forward, causing the home defence – and Baker – plenty of problems, as three times he was unlucky in front of goal, until six minutes from time he moved smoothly from right to left before crashing a shot past the Everton keeper. A minute later and this remarkable match took what some thought would be a final twist, with the Scot, Johnny Duncan, putting Leicester 4-3 ahead.

But just when the day couldn't get any worse for Everton, it unfortunately did. Two minutes from time the referee awarded the home team a penalty. Alec Troup, in what was his only spot-kick for the club, struck the ball well but saw it bounce off the crossbar and into the crowd. Moments later the referee blew for full time. Those present could not comprehend what they had witnessed; the Blues had thrown away a three-goal lead and missed a crucial penalty in the same match. Unbelievable.

POSTSCRIPT:

The pre-Christmas period in this season was one for unusual and unexpected comebacks in Everton matches. A 1-0 lead at home to Newcastle in October became a 3-1 loss. The following week at Leeds the reverse happened. Derby County in November saw a 2-0 deficit turned into a 3-2 win and three weeks later a 3-1 lead at Aston Villa was frittered away with the home team victorious 5-3.

Two 5-4 defeats to Leicester – in the same season

Everton were relegated for the first time from the top-flight in season 1929-30. Two games that contributed to their demise were both nine-goal thrillers against the same opponents who had turned around the three-goal deficit in 1926. To say the game at Goodison on November 30th 1929 was see-saw would be an understatement. Everton went 2-0 up through Rigby and Martin only to find themselves 5-2 down a minute after half-time. But goals by Rigby and Tommy White got it back to 5-4, just after the hour, but the visitors held-on in conditions 'so dark at the end it was impossible to see the players.'

At Filbert Street in April there was a familiar tale. Everton were down 3-1 just before half-time and then found themselves 4-3 ahead with 15 minutes left, only to see their nemesis from 1926, Arthur Chandler, equalise to complete his hat-trick and then lay on Len Barry's winner three minutes from time.

The greatest-ever comeback by an Everton team

This came in January 1995. A FA Youth Cup tie at Goodison was the stuff of nightmares after half-an-hour. A not especially strong Blackpool side were 4-0 up until Graham Allen pulled one back before the break, and then the crowd were given further hope by a penalty from Matt Woods to further reduce the deficit. Nevertheless when the visitors scored again to make it 5-2 with 20 minutes left, all optimism had disappeared. But our close geographical neighbours were not the first to patent three-goal comebacks, and in the space of three minutes Everton came back to make it 5-5 with a treble burst from Weathers, Townsend and a second from Allen. On 87 minutes the small number of spectators saw the incredulous revival completed when Allen popped up to score the winner, complete his hat-trick and produce the greatest comeback by any Everton side ever.

BeeBC

A radio first
Everton 2-1 Leeds United
First Division, 12th March, 1927

Everton have a bit of a track record when it comes to the BBC, the match at Arsenal in 1936 was the first broadcast live on television in this country and 19 years later the Toffees featured on the debut of *Saturday Sport Special*, which was the forerunner of *Match of the Day*. But radio broadcasting goes back even further, to 22nd January 1927 in fact, when the BBC broadcast coverage of the Arsenal and Sheffield United match from Highbury.

The *Radio Times* for that week showed a diagram of the pitch, divided into eight notional squares so that listeners could follow the progress of the game – the commentators describing play by saying which square the ball was in (this is thought to be the origin of the phrase 'back to square one').

After the success of this experiment other matches quickly followed – although not at Anfield, where the club refused permission on the grounds of the potential impact on attendances – and it was only a matter of time before Goodison saw its first wireless commentary. The game chosen was a home match against Leeds and the man selected to do the talking was none other than Ernest Edwards, sports editor of the *Liverpool Echo*.

As has already been seen, Edwards used the nom de plume 'Bee' for his newspaper reports. Bee was a slightly egotistical and eccentric character – he reported from what he called 'the Hive' – but there was no doubt that his colourful prose and persistent name-dropping (especially on glamorous away visits to London) added a bit of much-needed spice to football reporting in the grim years between the two World Wars. Edwards was once asked to referee a schoolboy match and he did so from the side of the playing area, atop a large ladder that he had brought especially, on the not unreasonable grounds that it provided a much clearer view of the play.

Without a doubt Edwards carried an enormous amount of cachet within local football, as the local press was perhaps the spectator's sole point of reference for considered opinion. Will Cuff, who himself was enormously influential at Everton during this period, also knew the value of keeping Edwards onside and both parties maintained a close working relationship. But Edwards was a shrewd operator and he was known to abuse this privilege, as exemplified in his role in the notorious Sam Chedgzoy affair in 1924, which was described earlier. The fact Cuff let Edwards, a journalist, into the inner sanctum of the players' dressing room at half-time indicates such a relationship was not always healthy.

However, on the big day there was bit of a problem. If Bee was doing the commentary, then who would do the *Liverpool Echo's* reporting? A compromise was reached and, in what must be a landmark moment for newspaper journalism, the Saturday *Football Echo* used the transcript of Bee's radio commentary for their match report!

As for the game itself, both teams were near the bottom of the table at the time with Everton giving a debut to Tony Weldon, a forward signed from Airdrie two days before. The week before had seen a 7-3 defeat in a real debacle at Newcastle so the size of the crowd - a remarkable 58,000, a record for the ground – was a real surprise. Bee began the game by announcing: 'It is just 3.15 and off they go. Everton are kicking off and Dean has passed the ball to Forshaw. It has now gone to the Leeds inside left…'. What was clear though was that both teams were understandably tense about their meeting; in Bee's words they 'are nervous and excited beyond words.'

The away team were having most of the play early on and threatened Taylor's goal on several occasions, although the commentary lacked the detail that would send any producer apoplectic today: 'Even so there off goes Jennings and very nearly scoring.' The home side remained in the game though and Bee described that rarest of moments: 'Here come Cresswell, Hart and Dean – a lovely movement, with Dean not more than five yards from the goal, but he has almost entirely missed the ball.'

What was clear was that Bee had decided, typically, to eschew the BBC's planned commentary style and at no point did he refer to any squares whatsoever, something that did indeed send the producer irate!

The Toffees were ragged and disjointed, especially Alec Troup ('not his dandy self today') and it was no surprise that Tom Jennings opened the scoring for the Yorkshire side 11 minutes into the second half. This stung – pardon the pun – the home side into action (in Bee's words: 'Can Everton fight? Can a bee buzz') and it was soon 1-1 when Weldon was pushed in the back in the

Leeds area. Dean stepped up and blasted the kick past the Leeds keeper.

That was just before the hour and there was now constant pressure applied to the Leeds defence with Potts in the opposition goal having a real blinder, despite being knocked out by 'a cannon ball' from Troup. But when Potts brought off a fine save from Dean, up stepped the new boy Weldon to knock in the rebound. The Blues continued to bombard the Leeds goal up to full time and only poor finishing from the forward line prevented them adding to their total.

The 2-1 win was crucial as it happened. Leeds finished 21st in the table and were relegated, with Everton finishing one place and four points above them. If the result had been reversed at Goodison though, they would have stayed up at the Blues' expense due to a better goal average. Everton would not have won the title in 1927-28 and, more importantly, Dixie Dean may not have scored his 60 goals. Funny old game eh?

POSTSCRIPT:

Of far more importance to Bee was the publicity surrounding his commentary. Never one to blow his own trumpet when you can hire a brass band do the job on your behalf, he printed some listeners' comments, after his match report, two days later:

Mr W. Thomas from Sefton Park: 'I have no doubt you will receive a large number of letters complimenting you on your broadcasting. At half-time, one of my guests turned to me and with a face beaming with pleasure remarked, 'I have never enjoyed anything so much in my life.' My heartiest congratulations for the great treat you gave us.'

A 'countryman' of Skelmersdale: 'Thank you for your splendid broadcasting message. I enjoyed it immensely.' Mr Alty 'took pleasure from hearing the game', and Mr Smith of Formby added: 'For all these people I say thank you.'

But Will Cuff, the Everton chairman at the time, divulged a slightly different tale a few years later. It appeared that Bee's complete disregard for the rules of commentary had not gone down well with the BBC hierarchy. Indeed, by half-time he was handed a note: 'Put the squares into the round holes of the commentary.'

But Bee being Bee took no notice. Although, as Cuff pointed out it was the *Liverpool Echo's* sport editor who led the subsequent change in commentary style: 'He was before his time, the BBC would now never dream of squaring any match – they have more sense than ruin the flow of comment by the interjection of 'Squares'.' But Bee never did another commentary.

The great man, William Ralph 'Dixie' Dean (above left) - a scorer against Leeds; an original George Green cartoon of Warney Cresswell (above right); an Everton team line-up, circa 1932 (below)

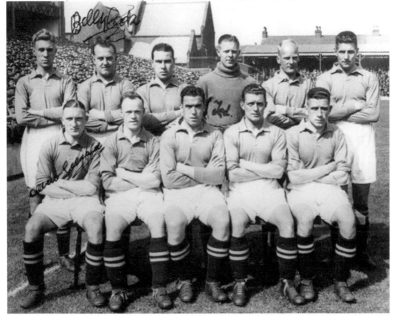

Fogg causes chaos

Referee awards four penalties
Blackburn Rovers 5-3 Everton
First Division, 25th December, 1931

O nly one match in this country has featured the award of five penalty kicks – on Easter Monday 1989, Crystal Palace missed three and scored one whilst Brighton scored one in their league fixture. But pre-dating that match was a remarkable game on Christmas Day 1931 when the British record of four spot-kicks in one match was equalled (one of those matches was the visit by Sheffield Wednesday to Goodison in March 1905, which was covered earlier).

Everton ventured to Ewood Park on top of the league, having been promoted as champions of Division Two the previous season. Dean was in one of the most productive spells of his career, having clocked up a truly astonishing 25 goals in 15 league matches since netting a hat-trick at Anfield in mid-September. His largesse resulted in the first 20 games of the season yielding 70 goals for the Toffees.

Blackburn went ahead after 12 minutes when Jack Bruton took advantage of a through ball – and the generosity of the referee, Mr Fogg of Bolton, who ignored the linesman's flag as the winger was apparently two yards offside – to shoot confidently past Sagar. Twenty minutes later the Blues were level, when Cliff Binns in the Rovers goal pulled down Dean as he was about to score yet another header. Mr Fogg awarded his first penalty of the afternoon and Tommy White netted easily.

The parity lasted just three minutes, Blackburn's McLean scoring one of the goals of the season from 35 yards out. But within a minute it was 2-2, Dean capitalizing on a mistake by Hutton to fire past the Rovers keeper. Shortly afterwards Everton went ahead for the only time in the game when Dean, moving swiftly in from the by-line saw his shot handled by Gorman and for the second time in the game, White scored from the spot.

But with the last kick of an exhilarating first half, Ernie Thompson equalized for the home side with a fine cross-shot past the helpless Sagar.

The teams went in at 3-3 at the break.

Into the second half Everton continued to be the more incisive of the two sides, their measured and cooler approach contrasting with the more rumbustious manner of the opposition. But midway through the half Thompson broke through from midfield and was brought down by Ted Sagar as he tried to round the keeper. Sagar made amends from Hutton's spot-kick, diving full length to tip it spectacularly around the post. It was the third penalty awarded by Mr Fogg.

Although the dangerous Dean was well shackled by the impressive Imrie, the away team continued to have the better of the action as the game entered the final five minutes. But drama was to follow, as a cross from the Rovers right was clearly brought down by Groves' hand before the Rovers forward drove home to take the score to 4-3. For the second time in the afternoon, the referee chose to ignore the flagging linesman and awarded a goal.

Then Mr Fogg, who had not done the away team any favours all afternoon, made it a trio of poor decisions against the Toffees by mysteriously awarding a penalty after Sagar had dived and saved at Bruton's feet. Despite protests from Everton, he refused to explain his decision and McLean rubbed salt in an already large wound by beating the keeper. And that was that: four penalty kicks awarded and the Christmas Day presents given to the home side turned a probable win for the Blues into a barely believable 5-3 defeat. But Everton would have the last laugh both on the following day and at the end of the season.

POSTSCRIPT:

In spite of a bit of daylight robbery at Ewood Park on Christmas Day 1931, Everton cruised towards their fourth league title the following spring, finishing two points ahead of Arsenal. But before that came a return match against Rovers on Boxing Day at Goodison, and a 53,000 crowd saw a 5-0 hammering that made up for the injustices of the previous afternoon. Dean was the star man with a hat-trick and he was the top scorer at the season's end – with 45 league goals, the third-highest ever in the top flight, but it barely warrants a mention against his momentous 1927-28 achievements.

Everton matches to feature three penalties

Everton 8 Darwen 1 - 21st October 1893

Everton thrash Darwen despite the away team being awarded two
spot-kicks, one being scored by James Orr after Bob Howarth had saved
John McKnight's first effort in the opening period. The great Jack
Southworth easily converted his kick for Everton.

Derby County 1 Everton 4 - 18th September 1912

The Blues romp to their usual win at Derby, with John Maconnachie
opening the scoring with a penalty after half an hour. Seven minutes later
the same player has another chance from the spot, but shoots straight at the
Derby keeper although he manages to knock the rebound in. The Everton
defender then handles two minutes from time, only to see the great Steve
Bloomer – whose league goalscoring record was broken by Dixie Dean –
shoot against the underside of the bar and out again.

Man City 6 Everton 2 - 7th December 1957

Two top-flight records are set at Maine Road when Ken Barnes (father of
Peter) becomes the first player to record a hat-trick of penalties in a
top-flight game. Jimmy McAdam of City sets a new post-War scoring record
of netting in 10 consecutive league games. Dave Hickson is also sent off for
dissent to complete a miserable afternoon for the Blues.

Everton 3 Tottenham 2 - 14th March 1970

Welsh centre-half Mike England – who later would be linked with the
Everton manager's post in the dark days of 1983-84 - becomes only the
second player to concede two penalties in the same game at Goodison. Five
minutes from half-time his foul on Royle results in a penalty, scored by Alan
Ball. On the hour he fells the same player, but this time Pat Jennings pushed
the ball around the right-hand post. In a tight game Bond levels from the
spot at 2-2 before Joe Royle scored the winner.

Crystal Palace 2 Everton 3 - 28th February 1981

Match of the Day viewers see the last instance of two Everton players missing from the spot in the same match, Trevor Ross had his kick saved by Paul Barron five minutes before half-time, and then on 52 minutes Steve McMahon fired wide. Clive Allen had more success after 77 minutes when he coolly slotted home, but the Blues held on for their final away win under Gordon Lee. Coincidentally Joe McBride also missed from the spot for the reserves on the same afternoon.

Dario Gradi was Crystal Palace manager on the day, and he was not impressed when chairman Ron Noades put all the Palace players on the transfer list before Everton had left the ground.

Reykavik 2 Everton 3 - 14th September 1995

The Blues' first foray into Europe for 10 years sees the referee from Luxembourg, Roger Phillippe, award three penalties. Two were given to the home side and were both converted by Mihajilo Bibercic whilst David Unsworth scored his kick for the away team. There have been only six penalties awarded in Everton matches in Europe, and all six have been away from home, with Iceland seeing four of them (Joe Royle missed his kick against Keflavik in 1970).

Everton 2 Newcastle 2 - 13th September 2003

Refereee Rob Styles manages to book ten and order Gary Naysmith and Laurent Robert off at Goodison in what was not a particularly dirty encounter. He also awards two penalties to Newcastle, both converted by Alan Shearer past debutant Nigel Martyn, and three minutes from time Duncan Ferguson equalizes from the spot with his first goal for the club in 18 months.

Other dodgy referees

Mr Barton, Everton v Chelsea, 15th April 1933

'A sensational end to the half' according to the *Liverpool Echo* as Tommy Johnson nods into the net as the referee blows his whistle for half-time. After a heated argument the man in the middle would not change his decision.

Unknown referee, Everton v Southport, 13th October 1949

A Liverpool Senior Cup match between the two sides at Goodison was heading comfortably in the way of the visitors when a shot by Russell beat Ted Sagar in the Everton goal and rebounded back out from the rear of the net. The referee did not award the goal, even though it clearly went at least six foot behind the line.

Mr Jackson, Plymouth Argyle v Everton, 15th November 1952

The Toffees had a couple of bad-tempered games on the South West coast in the dark days of Division Two during the 1950s. One, a 4-0 loss in October 1953, was described as a 'wrestling match' in the *Liverpool Echo*, whilst the other, a 1-0 defeat 12 months earlier, was the scene of one of those unfortunate refereeing clangers that has dogged the club over the years. Everton had never lost to Argyle in a first-team game and that record looked to be safe when with five minutes left the match was goalless. Then Neil Dougal of the home side started a run from just inside the Everton half, one that was halted by a tackle by George Cummins. Mr Jackson clearly blew for a foul and all the players stopped - apart from Dougal that is, who in a fit of pique carried on and drove the ball into the net from 40 yards out. Ted Sagar made a late attempt to save a shot that he would have stopped with comparative ease had he wanted to. Then, to everyone's astonishment, the referee awarded a goal. 'Quite how he justified his decision will probably remain a mystery forever' was the *Daily Post's* view, and despite being surrounded by Everton players he was not for turning. Plymouth kept hold of their lead to record their first win against Everton, although even their directors, players and supporters agreed that the Blues had been hard-done by.

Mr Webb, Everton v Portsmouth, 13th December 1958

'Erratic' would be the simplest way of describing the said official's handling of this league match at Goodison, which saw Everton put one over their South Coast bogey side. Having suffered more than their fair share of bad luck in a recently-ended league-record run of 13 consecutive defeats at the hands of Pompey, the Toffees more than balanced things up in a game they won 2-1. After Eddie Thomas had scored from a clearly offside position, Portsmouth were denied a second equaliser on the stroke of half-time in an episode that had echoes of an infamous incident involving Billy Liddell at Anfield two years before. Ironically it was Ron Saunders, the former Everton centre-forward who was to resign as Norwich manager in unusual circumstances 15 years later (see Match 34), who was the victim of some stringent refereeing. Right on half-time he struck a ferocious shot which fizzed past Dunlop into the net, only to see it struck off as the referee had blown up just after he had touched the ball. The authorities at the time had introduced a new diktat of 'thou shalt not argue with the referee', which fortunately for Mr Webb meant that the complaints were a trickle, rather than a flood.

The second half was ludicrously the opposite, Mr Webb erroneously playing 90 seconds over the allotted time until the linesman reminded him to blow the whistle.

Mr Harper, Stoke City v Everton, August 29th 1965

John Hurst was a long and valued servant for the club in over 400 first-team games, but for him personally few could have lived up to the drama that surrounded his debut. Having made history as the first-ever Everton substitute in this game, when coming on for Fred Pickering seven minutes from time, he nearly became the first to score when his well-struck shot came back off the inside of the post. At the end of the match Hurst, like everyone else, definitely thought he had that record when heading what looked to be the winner from a corner. The referee, Mr Harper, had other ideas, blowing the whistle as the player made contact in a manner that was repeated by Clive Thomas in the Brazil v Sweden World Cup clash 13 years later. Despite protestations from all the away team, Harper was unmoved: 'I was looking at my watch as the corner-kick was taken. Standing at the near post I watched the ball passing my face and then blew for full time. No doubt it was unfortunate for Everton but time was up and that was that.' Ouch!

Pen taken three times

Roy Vernon's penalty against Manchester United in the FA Charity Shield match at Goodison in August 1963 was a saga in its own right. After the referee, Mr Crawford, had awarded a penalty for a Maurice Setters foul on the Welshman, the Everton captain was about to strike the ball when it was noticed that Dave Gaskell, the United keeper, was two yards off his line. Vernon stopped before he shot and Noel Cantwell, the United skipper, raced over to the ref to protest and was promptly booked. When the kick was retaken Vernon put the ball to Gaskell's left and the keeper made a fine save. But the linesman flagged that Cantwell had stepped into the penalty area, so the kick was ordered to be taken for a third time. On this occasion Vernon slid the ball to the keeper's right for the second goal in a 4-0 win.

Roy Vernon, third-time lucky in the 1963 FA Charity Shield against Manchester United

Whitewashed ball

Woodwork struck eight times
Bolton Wanderers 2-4 Everton
First Division, 8th April, 1933

Every so often comes a match where just the plain reporting of the facts is sufficient to reflect the passage of play. Everton's victory at Bolton, just three weeks before the FA Cup was lifted by the Blues for the first time at Wembley, falls firmly into that category.

The Toffees ventured to Burnden Park having enjoyed an inconsistent season in the league, although the recent win over West Ham had secured a place in the FA Cup final. Just five of the previous 17 league matches had been won, but the 27 goals scored in those five games was testimony to the side's wayward form. Dean was having a lean spell by his towering standards – his end-of-season tally would stand at 24 league goals or just over half of the previous year – whilst the ageing team around him struggled to match the title-winning performances of 1931-32. Bolton were also struggling, and they would be relegated at the end of the season. The gate for the game was just over 10,000 in the spring sunshine – the nearby Holcombe races proving to be a greater attraction for the local population.

Hit the post

Straight from the kick-off, Jimmy Stein crossed dangerously into the Bolton goalmouth and when Harry Church, the home keeper, failed to gather the ball cleanly, two Everton players missed opportunities before inside-forward Jimmy McGourty headed onto the home crossbar. Two minutes later Geldard did well to force the Bolton full-back, Finney, into conceding a throw-in and from his resulting centre Bolton's Mike Boyle sliced the clearance into his own net. 1-0 to the visitors.

After 10 minutes Bolton equalized. Good work on the left enabled McKay to centre and Jack Milsom bundled the ball over the line. Two minutes later there was further drama in the Everton box, this time a cross by Rimmer was flayed at by Sagar and the ball fell kindly to Cook who, from three yards out, shot tamely and that fine full-back, Warney Cresswell, cleared off the line.

Hit the post

It was Everton's turn to press, and after 'Tosh' Johnson had shot just over when well placed, Dean shot sharply from just inside the area and the Bolton keeper, Church, turned the ball onto the post and out of play.

Hit the bar and post

Shortly after a fine cross by Stein was met with a powerful header by Dean and the ball crashed against the bar and then McGourty struck the rebound against the post. Both players had hit the woodwork twice, and the game was not even half-an-hour old!

After 25 minutes, Everton went ahead, a well judged cross by Cliff Britton was met with characteristic power by Dean, and he left Church helpless with a perfect header.

Hit the post twice

Just after the half-hour mark the woodwork was struck again twice in quick succession - this time both Jimmy Stein and Jock Thomson struck the post for the visitors. Before half-time though Bolton equalized when the dangerous Milsom, the best player on the pitch by some distance, crossed to Cook and his header could only be pushed out by Sagar to Rimmer, who scored easily.

Hit the post

The second half followed exactly the same pattern as the opening period. In the first minute Albert Geldard beat four men and it was now his turn to strike the upright – the winger's shot rebounding off the Bolton post and bouncing out to safety.

The Blues had to wait just five minutes to regain the lead nevertheless, Jock Thomson chipping in from the left for Dean to head home. It was the great man's 28th goal of the season. Everton went 4-2 ahead moments later and appropriately it was McGourty - who, like Dean had already struck the woodwork twice - who found the net from a Jimmy Stein cross. For reasons best known to himself, McGourty wore his jersey back to front for the game.

Hit the bar

Bolton were still fighting hard, and for the second time in the game Cresswell was required to clear off the line from Cook and, after Sagar had saved well from Milsom's header, Cook struck the rebound against the crossbar. It was remarkably the eighth time the crossbar or post had been struck in the opening hour of the game. According to the *Liverpool Echo*, the ball was now covered in whitewash from the amount of times it had struck the woodwork.

The Blues continued to press hard and showed no signs of easing up on account of the forthcoming date at Wembley. 'Tosh' Johnson went close on a couple of occasions and Jimmy Stein, who was having an off day, wasted two good chances. At the other end Billy Cook clearly brought down Rimmer in the penalty area, but the Blues full-back was lucky to escape, and then Milsom had the ball in the net but was ruled marginally offside.

Everton held on to their 4-2 lead, but these two decisions clearly riled the home crowd who gave the referee, Mr A. Kingscott (Long Eaton) 'a severe reception' according to the *Daily Post* at the end of the game.

POSTSCRIPT:

The eight occasions the ball hit the woodwork in this match is a record for an Everton game. To put this in perspective, in the whole of the 2005-06 season Everton struck the woodwork just seven times. In fact the 1932-33 campaign had other interesting curiosities:

- Famously that year's FA Cup final was the first to feature numbered shirts, with the Toffees wearing 1-11. Amazingly Everton had over 250,000 applications for tickets.

- Three weeks before the final Everton unusually wore their white kit that would be used at Wembley for the home league match against Newcastle, for the sole purpose that the players could visually get used to their colleagues.

- Jimmy Stein scored direct from corner-kicks in both league matches against Sunderland.

Alec Shackleton had a lot on his plate when he returned to the Everton side in November 1959 for the home game against Leicester. Not only was he under pressure from the crowd for a string of disappointing performances after his arrival from Leeds, but he had been moved to centre-forward to displace the dropped Dave Hickson. (Indeed, this was the match when a spectator ran onto the pitch with a sign: 'If Dave goes we all go' following speculation that he had played his last game for the club.)

Shackleton must have thought it was going to be one of those days when, in the opening 30 seconds, he remarkably struck both the bar and then the post. From the kick-off he sent a crunching left-foot shot against the crossbar and a right-footed shot moments later bounced off the base of the upright. But Alec kept going and he was rewarded with a fine goal in a 6-0 victory. But he failed to settle at Goodison and moved on 18 months later. As for the 'Cannonball Kid' – he never played for the club again.

In the course of a 2-0 win over Sheffield United reserves on 21st October 1961, Everton reserves struck the crossbar on four occasions in the first 20 minutes.

Alec Shackleton in action (above left) - his performances for Leeds persuaded the Blues to bring him to Goodison Park. He replaced Dave Hickson (above right) at centre-forward against Newcastle United in November 1959, and the 'Cannonball Kid' would never play for Everton again

A Strange Start

Filbert Street fiasco
Leicester City 3-1 Everton
First Division, 28th October, 1933

Delayed starts to football matches are not unusual. Even the World Cup final has not been averse to the odd debacle – like the gamesmanship involving the Argentineans in the 1978 final, when their protests over the protective bandage covering Rene van de Kerkhof's arm held up the kick-off, and four years earlier the start was delayed when referee Jack Taylor noticed an essential piece of equipment was missing – the corner flags!

What sets apart Everton's visit to Filbert Street in 1933 was that the kick-off was delayed on three different occasions, due to completely unrelated events. The Toffees were in mid-table at the time as an ageing team generally struggled, and they would ultimately have a fruitless campaign, with 15 out of the 42 league matches being drawn.

In those days due to the vagaries of public transport it was not unusual for teams or match officials to arrive at the last minute – indeed on several occasions Everton had to actually change in taxis on the way to the ground (see later in this passage). And on this day the beginning of the game was initially delayed as a linesman was late due to a rail problem, and this was despite him actually getting dressed whilst on the train – no doubt a fully clothed match official on public transport was slightly unusual.

After the linesman had arrived and when the players were making their way through the tunnel, Everton's Albert Geldard slipped and injured his leg, although luckily his hands were able to hold onto the wall and break his fall - but he was still allowed treatment in the dressing room. When the players finally made it onto the pitch the other linesman, on checking the goals, discovered that there was a hole in one of the nets! Club officials then had to do some running repairs while the players waited around in the cold.

The delayed start obviously affected the players' concentration, for both sides scored in the opening four minutes. After two minutes the Leicester inside-right Arthur Maw struck, lashing a terrific shot to the right of the helpless Sagar. But within 60 seconds of the kick-off the away side had equalized. Stein broke free on the right and McLaren, the Leicester keeper, could only palm the ball out to the waiting Tommy White who knocked the ball in with the goalkeeper helpless on the ground.

Leicester restored their lead on 10 minutes, when Danny Liddle's cross was missed by everyone and Hugh Adcock nipped in at the far post to score from close range. There was no doubt that the delayed start had unsettled the teams, especially Everton, whose defence looked unusually shaky. This was again the case after a quarter of an hour, when they stopped to let the ball cross the goal-line only to see Adcock retrieve the ball when still in play and his cross was met by Campbell from three yards out. The remainder of the half saw the home side generally on top with Arthur Lochhead causing Everton constant problems.

The second half was the complete opposite to what had gone before, with McLaren saving what would have been an own goal from Jones and then Adam Black kicked off the line from a Billy Cook free-kick. Everton continued to press, with the Foxes breaking only spasmodically, and Jimmy Dunn went close as did the struggling Geldard (who was clearly feeling the effects of his pre-match fall).

Near the end of the second half came a comical ending to match the comical start of the game. A throw-in was taken by the Leicester right-back Black to the goalkeeper, who promptly slipped up and fell into the mud leaving Jimmy Dunn with an open goal but the Everton forward, whose form had been patchy, managed to screw his shot wide. Although Everton continued to press they failed to breach the Leicester rearguard and the home side held on for a deserved victory thanks to their blistering opening spell. But the match will be remembered for the slightly bizarre beginning!

Other strange starts

Broken goals, Birmingham City (h), 27th December 1924

Everton rushed home from their Boxing Day match at Newcastle to discover the start delayed at Goodison. Heavy overnight gales had caused the tarpaulins covering both goals to break free, taking the goalposts with them. The directors (!), with help from the groundstaff, repaired the damage whilst the players hung around on the pitch. The referee bizarrely blew the whistle when he was happy with their work so that the game could commence, some 10 minutes after the scheduled start.

The worst fixture planning ever, Plymouth (h), 27th December 1930

This is not so much about the start of the game, more the preparations. In what was the most preposterous example of bad planning, Plymouth were asked over the holiday period to play away at Everton, less than 24 hours after finishing a home match in the South West. A long train journey of 300 miles followed, which started at midnight and ended at Lime Street at 6am in the morning. The players slept until 1pm before going to Goodison. Not surprisingly they were the proverbial lambs to the slaughter, going down 9-1 with Dean and Jimmy Stein both netting four goals.

Heads or tails? Southport (h, FA Cup), 28th February 1931

Although the impact on the start time was minimal, the largest cheer before the start of this Cup-tie at Goodison was reserved for the winning of the toss, as the rain-sodden pitch meant the referee and two captains needed five attempts to resolve the issue, as the coin continually got stuck in the mud.

Fog on the line, Birmingham City (a), 21st December 1935

Ten minutes before the scheduled kick-off and the spectators are still waiting, shivering in the cold outside of St. Andrew's. The reason being that there's no sign of the visitors – when Everton eventually turn-up it transpires that they have been delayed an hour through fog at Manchester and then at Crewe. 'Taxis to St. Andrew's' could be heard outside of New Street Station as the team – who had dressed in the station – climb into minicabs on their way to the ground. The game kicked off 20 minutes late and the visitors lose 4-2.

Kick-off brought forward, Portsmouth (h), 17 September 1946

The start of the match against Pompey was brought forward by 10 minutes, so the away side could catch the 5.25pm train from Lime Street!

Fire in press box, Blackpool (a), 4th November 1950

If it happened today then there might be rejoicing in certain quarters of the game, but such was the concern over a fire breaking out in the press area at Bloomfield Road, just before the kick-off, that it warranted the attention of three fire engines. Thankfully damage was minimal, with the press and crowd treated to a goal after just 30 seconds by the home team's Jackie Mudie. Forty-five years earlier members of the Fourth Estate had an even more uncomfortable afternoon at Preston. The away game on 9th September 1905 saw the rain drive down with harsh persistency, and thanks to a 'generously leaking roof' the press 'were altogether in a sorry plight.'

Everton impersonators, New South Wales XI (a), 2nd May 1964

Everton enjoyed a hugely successful tour of the Antipedes in May 1964, but a 4-1 win in front of a massive gate of 52,000 over a NSW side did not have the most straightforward of beginnings. The visitors were late arriving and a gang of students, some dressed in blue, came onto the pitch via the usual entrance pretending to be Everton. The crowd cheered but the local police, realising they had been duped, ran onto the pitch to remove the imposters. In the mêlée one was brought down with a 'flying tackle.' The game also featured an interesting bit of trivia concerning Matt Woods, a centre-half who had played for Everton in the previous decade before enjoying a highly successful time at Blackburn. Woods was playing with Sydney at the time and guested for the state side, the defender showed his true loyalties though by putting through his own net in the second period.

Matt Woods is sent off by referee L. Tirebuck for Blackburn against Everton in March 1959, with Dave Hickson lying prone on the ground. Woods was the first former player sent off against Everton and five years later he would be lining up against the Blues 'Down Under'

White Hartbreak Lane

Footballing myth exposed
Tottenham Hotspur 4-3 Everton
FA Cup fifth-round replay, 22nd February, 1937

White Hart Lane, like the other grounds in North London, has never been the happiest of hunting grounds for the Toffees. Although a 2-0 win in August 2006 was much deserved, recent years have mainly seen a series of disappointing results - but nothing sticks in the throat as much as this FA Cup defeat 70 years ago.

The teams had drawn 1-1 at Goodison in a disappointing match two days before when a bad-tempered game – 'a brawl' according to the *Liverpool Echo* - was poorly handled by the referee Mr Barton. Five minutes from time Arthur Rowe tripped Dean, who was clearly outside of the playing area behind the goal, and the referee awarded a penalty. Dean – described by Bee as having the 'quietest game he has ever experienced' – took the kick himself and justice was done when Jack Hall in the Spurs goal comfortably saved his shot. Two minutes from the end of the game McCormick put the London side ahead but Jackie Coulter equalized in the last minute.

For the replay two days later Everton mixed things around: Coulter was dropped and, with Alex Stevenson absent with flu, Tommy Lawton came in unusually at inside-left with Albert Geldard on the right wing. Lawton had been bought from Burnley in the January for £6,500 as a 17-year-old with a man's physique (as a 16-year-old amateur he was the heaviest member of the Turf Moor staff at nearly 13 stone). The centre-forward had scored on his debut for the Blues the week before in a 7-2 reverse at Molineux, to become both the club's youngest-ever player and scorer. Earlier in the season he had scored a hat-trick against Spurs for Burnley just after his 17th birthday, the youngest in league history to achieve the feat at the time.

Spurs were halfway down the Second Division, although they had a few useful players in Johnny Morrison, who scored 90 goals in 134 league games for the club and Vic Buckingham, who would later coach successfully abroad and when manager of Ajax was credited with discovering Johan Cruyff. Buckingham was also manager of Sheffield Wednesday in the infamous match at Ipswich Town in 1962 that led to the ban on Tony Kay. There was also a new referee, Mr Mee, after both sides had complained about Mr Barton's performance at Goodison. He too was to play an integral part in proceedings.

Conditions for the game were poor. The playing area was flooded on the morning of the game and although the ground staff had cleared most of the water, the pitch was still greasy and heavy come kick-off. The Blues started well and after just six minutes a cross from Geldard fell at the far post to Lawton, who shot first time into the roof of the net. Everton continued to dominate and Geldard, having perhaps his finest game in an Everton shirt, was giving the Spurs full-back Billy Whatley a torrid time, and after 20 minutes he reached the by-line and his pin-point cross was met by Dean, who finished clinically via the right-hand post to put the visitors two-up.

Seven minutes later Spurs were back in the game when Miller's throughball was finished powerfully from just outside the box by Morrison. Spurs were now in the ascendancy and Sagar had to save well again from the same player, but then Geldard again got to the by-line and his cross appeared to be headed into the open goal by Dean, but the ball stuck in the mud on the goal-line and was cleared. Two minutes from half-time Dean was again foiled by Hall, this time his sharp back-heel in the six-yard box bringing a fine reflex save.

The second half began with Everton still in the driving seat until an odd incident occurred which has been the cause of a bit of football mythology (see Postscript). Joe Mercer took a throw-in and the linesman immediately flagged for a foul throw, as the ball had gone out. But the referee allowed play to continue and the assistant lowered his flag. Torry Gillick was immediately brought down in the Spurs penalty area and referee Mee had no hesitation in awarding a penalty. Cue pandemonium. The home players virtually frog-marched Mee in the direction of the linesman, who obviously said enough for the referee to change his mind and award Spurs a throw-in. All this happened on the hour mark.

The match was now end-to-end and not for the first time a referee, after making one poor decision, balanced things up at the other end. Morrison's header was ruled out on account of an unidentified push on Sagar. Everton though did not have long to wait to go further ahead, with Dean making it 3-1 from close range after 66 minutes. Two minutes later a Meek pass found

Morrison and the forward coolly placed it past Sagar, although according to *The Times*, 'to many people less well placed than the referee he appeared to be offside.'

The away team held out for 20 minutes in the face of a barrage of Spurs attacks and still looked dangerous on the break, with Geldard and Britton (who played beautifully throughout) outstanding. But four minutes from time, with the Blues in sight of the finishing line, Morrison fed Meek and the forward took his opportunity to grab the equalizer. Two minutes later and the unthinkable happened. According to *The Times*, 'amid enthusiasm, legitimate frenzy and the general atmosphere of improbable fiction,' Miller swept down the right wing and there was Morrison to complete his hat-trick with a fine header. The Blues had lost a two-goal lead in the space of 20 minutes. Even then Dean blazed straight at Hall in the final seconds when well placed.

Against all the odds Spurs had won and the players were carried off the field by members of the 47,000 crowd.

POSTSCRIPT:

The really interesting bits happened after the game. As Everton licked their wounds on the train home Will Cuff, the club chairman, announced to the press that an attempt had been made to bribe Ted Sagar before the game at Goodison. A letter had been sent to the England international offering him £50 (a not insignificant sum at the time) 'to lose' the match. The letter bore a Mansfield postmark and although there were some investigations, no further action was taken.

Of far greater significance was a tale that surrounded this match for many years. The original source is unknown, but it may have been Will Cuff himself. Interviewed in 1949, Cuff recalled the incident with the penalty (or in his case a goal) that never was:

'The oddest delayed goal in my long history was that at Spurs' ground when at least three minutes after we had scored a goal the ball was taken to the far-distant part of the field for a throw-in which the linesman had not been able to force upon the referee.'

In his 1966 book *The Great Ones*, Joe Mercer nominated this match as the most memorable he played in during his long career (even ahead of captaining Arsenal to a 2-0 win over Liverpool in the 1950 FA Cup final).

Whether he was influenced by Cuff is unclear but he wrote the following account of the end of the game:

'Five minutes from the end of the game we were leading 3-1 and it looked a dead cert that Everton would go into the next round...then came a penalty in our favour. Arthur Rowe was ruled to have fouled Billy Dean...but after protests Mr Barton was persuaded to consult a linesman...who said the ball was out of play before it had been centred.'

This obviously does not reflect the reality of the game, and Joe had fused the penalty awarded at Goodison in the first match with the one given at Spurs but, never letting the facts get in the way of a good story, many publications repeated the tale as the actual story of the game.

Even Dixie Dean, in his fabled 1971 interviews with Michael Charters of the *Liverpool Echo* recounts a similar tale: 'With a few minutes to go we were leading 3-1...I was brought down and it was a clear penalty...the linesman said that the ball had gone out of play and the referee gave a throw-in to Spurs...from that throw-in they scored to make it 3-2 and they got two more to beat us 4-3.'

A real *Boys Own* tale of how a side 3-1 down with four minutes left, and facing a penalty, came back to win in normal time. But unfortunately it did not happen that way.

Dixie Dean in action against Spurs in 1937 - his last FA Cup game for the club

Ted's Excellent Adventure

Goalie's extraordinary day
Everton 3-0 Leicester City
First Division, 26th December, 1937

When you play nearly 500 games for a club in nearly 23 years there is always going to be the odd experience to tell the grandchildren about. Ted Sagar certainly had his fair share of unusual moments during his prolonged career, but none came close to his exploits of Boxing Day 1937.

The goalkeeping legend made his Everton bow in January 1930 in a 4-0 win over Derby and whilst at Goodison he won both League Championship and FA Cup honours, as well as four England caps. He holds the record for the longest period of time any player has stayed with one club side.

Ted was in his prime at the end of the decade, but the 1937-38 season was not a particularly fruitful one for the Blue half of Merseyside, with only the burgeoning talent of a young Tommy Lawton adding a spark to a term where the final league position was 14th and when the FA Cup saw a fourth-round exit to Sunderland.

In the days when fixtures were played on both Christmas and Boxing Days, it was standard practice to play the same club on both, so the game against Leicester was the reverse to the one played at Filbert Street 24 hours previously, where the Foxes had overpowered the visitors 3-1.

Sagar had in fact just returned the day before from a long absence due to a fourth cartilage operation, the *Liverpool Echo* commenting that he was not the luckiest keeper in terms of injuries, comparing him to the great Frank Swift, who had not missed a game in four seasons at Manchester City.

The first half was a cagey affair according to reports, with Everton quite happy to give the opposition the ball, but Leicester, for all their possession, were unable to produce one single scoring opportunity, with Torry Gillick, Robert 'Bunny' Bell and Nat Cunliffe all spawning good chances for the home side. The game changed just before half-time when a ball put through the Everton backline was picked up by Liddle whose cross was gathered by

Sagar, just as Joe Mercer was about to kick clear - the result being an injured shoulder for the Blues' keeper, courtesy of the right boot of his team-mate. After a brief, but heated discussion between the players it was decided that centre-forward Bell should take over in goal, but while a replacement was sought a spectator ran onto the pitch and plonked himself in the goal, only to be escorted from the ground by the local constabulary. The *Liverpool Echo's* statement that 'he could have kept goal so paltry was the City shooting' was accurate though.

At half-time Sagar was taken to the nearby Stanley Hospital for treatment where his shoulder, which was in fact dislocated, was put back in place. During his absence at the start of the second period the opposition, whose delicate approach play produced little in the way of end product, rarely troubled his replacement. On the other hand the home side showed more drive and flair than previous and they gained their reward 12 minutes into the half, when Gillick's corner kick was met perfectly by Lawton.

Shortly after, the crowd gasped in disbelief when the injured Sagar returned to the field. He didn't return to the goal but was placed, after much confusion and aimless running around on his behalf, on the left wing, purely for nuisance value. From goalkeeper to hospital to outside-left in the space of just over 30 minutes, it was certainly an interesting afternoon for the Goodison custodian!

The arrival of Sagar clearly boosted the home team who went 2-0 ahead when Dougie Trentham fired past McLaren in the Leicester goal. The Everton keeper did not disgrace himself on the left and indeed he nearly scored, firing wide when well placed shortly after the goal. Nine minutes from time Lawton scored his second of the day, finishing well after good work by Mercer.

That completed the scoring, but although Lawton's display of the forward's arts was impeccable, the real hero was the brave Everton keeper, who displayed great courage in helping his team-mates. Although he didn't find the net, other goalkeepers have done so at the ground.....

POSTSCRIPT:

Sixty-four years after Sagar, one keeper made Premiership history by netting from open play, Peter Schmeichel stealing the show by volleying past Paul Gerrard in the closing moments of a 3-2 home win over Aston

Villa in 2001.

But two years prior to Ted's heroics, Goodison had seen an even more remarkable goal from a keeper. During the first half of the match against the reigning league champions Arsenal, the opposition keeper Frank Moss injured his shoulder after punching the ball away with his side leading 1-0. Moss left the field and was replaced in goal by defender Eddie Hapgood.

Nobody expected Moss to come back and few realised that when the sides returned after the break, Hapgood was still between the sticks with Moss playing as a 'passenger' at outside-left. The keeper did little up until the 70th minute when he took a square pass from Ted Drake and fired past Sagar. Most spectators still thought that the actual scorer was the Gunners' celebrated winger Cliff Bastin, who had moved inside when Hapgood went in goal. Moss left the field shortly after due to his earlier injury, only to come back again after treatment.

After playing for a few minutes he then left for good, to the rather muted applause of the crowd. A couple of weeks later Moss returned to Goodison to receive the match ball as a gift from the club. The keeper's injury had other repercussions for Everton: to provide cover the Gunners bought reserve keeper George Bradshaw from the Toffees.

Ted's goal to forget

A Dixie Dean hat-trick was a highlight of the comfortable 4-1 home win over Huddersfield in March 1932. However the '1' was a source of much embarrassment to the Everton keeper. Sagar easily saved a second-half header but, after collecting the ball and in attempting to throw it out, he only succeeded in hurling the ball into the net in a manner to be repeated by Gary Sprake at Anfield many years later.

'A game full of reprisals'

The above was the description of a bad-tempered fixture at Wolves in September 1936, in which Ted had an integral role. An encounter that had little football in between 'prolonged bouts of kicking' saw Sagar as the target of terrace abuse throughout, and at the end a spectator got onto the playing area and tried to attack him; thankfully the miscreant was arrested. The game did, however, feature a comedy own goal from Reg Hollingworth of the home side, the centre-half deflecting Leyfield's cross into his own net, despite the best efforts of his team-mate Jack Nelson, who trod on the ball as it crossed the goal-line. The crowd also had some much-needed humour with the sight of Joe Mercer changing his shorts in the centre-circle. However, the game was, according to the *Daily Post*: 'Dangerous, dirty and beneath contempt.'

Andy Rankin on the wing

There has only been one instance in the post-War era of an Everton keeper playing as an outfielder during a first-team game. During the 1-1 draw against Stoke City in December 1964, Andy Rankin was injured whilst snatching the ball from Eric Skeels at the beginning of the second half, and the regular deputy of the time, Sandy Brown, went between the sticks.

The Everton keeper, who had suffered a small fracture in his right hand, returned to the pitch on the left wing for the final 20 minutes, although his impact was understandably limited. Ironically Brown was injured diving at a Stoke forward's feet and sustained an injury that kept him out of the team the following Saturday.

Gordon West in reserve

After dislocating his thumb at Goodison in the 2-2 draw against Bolton for Everton reserves in September 1964, the charismatic keeper played the rest of the game at centre-forward with outfielder George Sharples replacing him.

Nev's unusual double

The friendly against Borussia Moenchengladbach in July 1992 saw the great man at his eccentric best. Nev always fancied himself as an outfielder and he played in midfield for the final five minutes after Barry Horne went off injured, with the last substitute Jason Kearton playing in goal. Earlier the Welshman had saved a penalty from Schultz, so on the day he completed what may be a unique double. Some outfielders have saved a penalty after going in goal – but how many have done the reverse?

The Golden Penalty

Cup tie settled in unique manner
Everton 2-2 Preston North End
FA Cup third round, second leg, 11th January, 1946

Which side appeared in the FA Cup final after losing a game in an earlier round? The answer to this old chestnut is Charlton Athletic, who were beaten 4-1 by Derby County in the 1946 final. The reason - as an experiment, the first post-War cup competition was played over two legs and Charlton were beaten 2-1 by Fulham in the second leg of an earlier tie but still went through on aggregate. The 1946 final is also famous for the ball bursting, and the chances of this happening were discussed before the game by the match commentator (remarkably when the two teams met in the league a couple of days later, the ball burst in that match as well).

That season the organising committee decided to move to a two-legged tie following a meeting at the HQ of the Football Association on June 1st 1945. This was done to give all clubs a chance in the competition, as some were not fully equipped with sufficient players following wartime football. The important minute read:

'That the competition be run on the home and away principle from the first to the sixth rounds of the competition proper, and one game on the knock-out principle in the qualifying rounds and in the semi-final and final ties. In the event of a draw after the second leg, extra time shall be played, 10 minutes each way. If the result is still a draw, the tie to be played to a finish, the first goal scored determining the winner and terminating the tie.'

So, what happened to the mighty Blues that season? Everton were drawn against Preston North End in the third round, with the first game scheduled for Deepdale and the return at Goodison.

The two teams lined up at Preston on the first Saturday of 1946 for the first official club fixture for seven years, following the ending of hostilities. The Lancashire team featured one Bill Shankly, whose rivalry off the pitch with the Blues was some 13 years away. Preston also had George Mutch, whose last-minute penalty had won the 1938 final, memorable for the match commentator stating just beforehand that he would eat his hat if one of the teams scored – and he did just that after the game.

The Blues included Harry Catterick, who was playing his first official game for the club, as well as Joe Mercer, which meant that the game had three of Merseyside's legendary footballing figures – and managers. They would all play an integral part in the way the tie developed.

Everton largely dominated the first encounter. Catterick scored six minutes into his debut following a centre from Wally Boyes. A quarter of an hour later there was an equalizer when centre-half John Humphreys' clearance struck keeper George Burnett and rebounded into the net. Little was seen of Preston until John Livesey scored what turned out to be the winner midway through the second half, in what was their only well-worked move of the match. The visitors furiously fought back, with the hard-working Catterick going close on three occasions, but the home side held on for a 2-1 victory.

The teams met at Goodison four days later. In what was described as the 'sternest cup-tie struggle seen at Goodison for many years,' the Blues continued to have the better of the play with winger Jim Rawlings – who had started his career at Preston 13 years previously and was fated never to play a league game for Everton – spurning several opportunities. It took just 17 minutes for Everton to take the lead on the day (and level the aggregate scores) when good work by Rawlings and Tommy Elliott, who also never played a league game for the club, resulted in a cross being handled by Scott. The referee Mr Ward pointed immediately to the spot and Joe Mercer calmly stuck the kick away.

The match continued on a heavy pitch and in blustery conditions and, apart from Rawlings, Catterick and Boyes also shot wide when placed. Preston also had their moments, but they were continually pegged back in their own half and it was a surprise that they kept the score down to just one goal at the end of 90 minutes.

Extra-time was played and curiously, after playing 90 minutes with just one goal scored, two came in the space of the opening five minutes. Elliott put Everton ahead on aggregate when he netted in a goalmouth scramble following a cross by Rawlings, despite the protestations of the opposition, who felt that Catterick had held down keeper Jack Fairbrother. Almost immediately Preston levelled when Jimmy McIntosh, who would later join Everton, scored the goal of the tie, a brilliant shot from just outside the box – helped by what was described as a half-hearted effort by Burnett.

After the allotted 20 minutes the score was 3-3 on aggregate, and in keeping with FA guidance it was decided that whilst the light was good the teams would play to a finish with the next goal being the 'winner.' The opening exchanges, like the previous four hours play, were bitterly contested until, with seven minutes played, a break from Preston saw Everton captain Norman Greenhalgh handle a goal-bound shot from Livesey. Although Dougal put the rebound back into the net, the referee had already blown for a penalty and from the resulting spot-kick it was Bill Shankly who executed the coup de grace by shooting firmly past Burnett.

The penalty immediately ended Everton's FA Cup hopes and for the only time in history a Toffees game was ended via a golden goal. Curiously it was only the second time a spot-kick had been scored against Everton at Goodison in the FA Cup – and there hasn't been one since.

POSTSCRIPT:

Owing to a few complaints from various clubs, such as the playing of extra time where necessary at the first time of asking - an obvious added advantage to the home side - and the suspension of midweek replays, a small but vital concession at a time when production and national recovery were always of premium importance, the rules altered at the FA's AGM in June 1946. The so-called 'special circumstances' were dropped and the competition went back to a straight knockout.

FA Cup penalties conceded at home

Just to confirm Shankly's place in Goodison FA Cup history, here is the full list of penalties taken against Everton in home games in the competition:

Harry Davis   **Sheffield Wednesday**   **10th March 1906**
Saved by Blues keeper Billy Scott after 20 minutes.

Harry Davis   **Sheffield Wednesday**   **10th March 1906**
Not to be outdone Davis nets in the second half, but Everton hang on for a 4-3 victory.

Bill Shankly **Preston North End** **9th January 1946**
Scored in sudden-death extra-time.

Henry Freeman **Fulham** **14th February 1948**
Ten minutes from the end of the game Freeman sends his spot-kick wide but
Fulham win 1-0.

Sam Lawrie **Charlton** **28th January 1959**
Lawrie's kick is sent wide of Dunlop's post in the second half. The miss
proves crucial as the Blues win 4-1 after extra-time on a foggy night in front
of 74,000.

Bill Leivers **Manchester City** **27th January 1962**
The City player's penalty is saved by Dunlop as the home side win
comfortably 2-0.

Bill Shankly (second left) celebrating Preston North
End's 1938 FA Cup final success. The Scot remains
the last player to score from the penalty spot
against Everton in the competition at Goodison Park

Raining cats and dogs

'Comedian dog and black cat'
Everton 2-1 Swansea Town
Second Division, 29th March, 1952

There certainly wasn't much to smile about on the Blue half of Merseyside - or the Red half for that matter - in the early 1950s; an air of despondency hung over the club following the Toffees' relegation from the top flight for only the second time in history. The depression was not lifted as the team, to be fair, showed no signs of escaping from Division Two. Matches against Liverpool, Manchester United and Arsenal were replaced by slightly less glamorous games against Brentford, Bury and Rotherham.

The highlights of the first season in the Second Division in 1951-52 were few and far between. The team struggled to adapt and a 1-1 draw at Luton in October 1951 saw the side plummet to the depths of 19th – the lowest league placing of any Everton side in history. The arrival of a young Dave Hickson as a striking regular saw an upturn in fortunes and by the time Swansea arrived at the end of March, the Blues were in the top-half of the table.

The Toffees line-up was virtually at full strength, with Hickson and John Willie Parker forging an increasingly fruitful partnership up-front, whilst behind them were the ball-playing skills of Wally Fielding and Tommy Eglington, as well as the durable Peter Farrell. In the Swansea side was that fine Welsh international Ivor Allchurch, who during the game was to set a unique and unwanted record. The fixture, played on a bleak, Arctic day in front of a 20,000 crowd was a classic, featuring several highly amusing and unusual incidents.

The Blues attacked first and Parker nearly scored with a header, as did Tony McNamara, before Swansea also went close when Medwin got through but was dispossessed by Clinton when certain to score. After a quarter of an hour though, the crowd had something to warm them up with the sight of a black terrier, which chased the ball around the pitch amongst the players for fully two minutes. Eventually the canine pitch invader caught up with the ball and the referee was forced to stop the match. But the fun didn't stop there as, according to press reports, the dog then produced a performing seal routine for the spectators, playfully balancing the ball on its nose and then entertaining the crowd with other tricks. It took the playful whistles of the onlookers to tempt him from the playing area.

The unexpected interruption disturbed the concentration of the players and shortly after the Welsh side went ahead with an unfortunate, but equally comical own goal. Their full-back Simmonds won the ball from Eglington and advanced purposefully down the right, his low cross arrowing in the direction of Blues' right-half Cyril Lello who, instead of clearing, tried to return the ball to keeper Jimmy O'Neill. The strong gale caused the ball to drift away from the centre of the goal and into the top corner, with the sight of the beaten O'Neill heavily colliding with the post adding a touch of farce.

Everton hit back immediately, with Parker striking a tremendous shot which just cleared the crossbar and Eglington had a shot cleared from the Swansea goal-line. Just before half-time the Blues earned rewards for their pressure though when Parker fired beyond King inside the far post.

Within five minutes of the re-start the Welsh side were awarded a penalty. A cross from the right drifted over keeper O'Neill and left Medwin with what was a simple opportunity to score, but Blues defender Jock Lindsay headed the ball off the line and then full-back Tommy Clinton pushed the rebound over the bar with his arm. Today such an act would result in an instant dismissal, but Clinton remained on the pitch. Ivor Allchurch took the resulting spot-kick, which unfortunately remains one of the worst seen at Goodison, the ball striking the upper deck of the Gwladys Street stand! Four months earlier the Welsh international had also struck his penalty wide in the game between the teams at the Vetch Field, and to this day he remains the only player to miss penalties in both league matches in a season against Everton.

Shortly after Goodison had a second unexpected visitor of the afternoon, in the form of a sleek black cat which ran on the pitch and, although not directly interfering with play like its canine friend in the opening half, certainly took the attention of the crowd away from the game whilst it swiftly darted around the playing area. After referee Mr Parkhurst stopped the match, the cat scurried from the pitch and amazed the watching crowd by jumping athletically over the gates at the Gwladys Street End of the ground.

Everton had the upper-hand and remarkably there was still time for another piece of history. On 70 minutes Lello struck a cross from the right with such ferocity that the Swansea keeper was unable to hang onto the ball and only succeeded in deflecting it into the net. The Blues midfielder had thus scored at both ends in the same match - the first time this had happened to an Everton player.

Swansea fought back well and although Allchurch was always a threat, the Blues defence remained firm. There was even time for more laughter from the crowd, as Wally Fielding was knocked out by a clearance as he raced away from goal - trainer Harry Cooke being required to administer the icy sponge. The Blues hung on, and when the final whistle came the small crowd celebrated, having seen certainly one of the funniest and most bizarre matches ever staged at Goodison.

POSTSCRIPT:

Remarkably this was not the only occasion Cyril Lello would score at both ends in an Everton game – he would also repeat the feat in the 5-2 win over Huddersfield at Goodison in November 1955. Derek Mountfield would also achieve this unusual feat on two occasions.

Everton scorers at both ends

Cyril Lello	v Swansea Town (h)	29th March 1952
Cyril Lello	v Huddersfield (h)	5th November 1955
Derek Mountfield	v Watford (a)	29th September 1984
Gary Stevens	v Sheffield Wed (h)	28th December 1985
Pat Van den Hauwe	v Blackburn (h) (FAC)	25th January 1986
Derek Mountfield	v Watford (h)	25th October 1986
Mike Newell	v Southampton (a)	16th March 1991
David Unsworth	v Newcastle (h)	3rd March 2001

Most penalties missed against Everton

3
Charlie Buchan (Sunderland)   1920-21, 1921-22 (2 in same game)

2
Alan Ball (Arsenal/Southampton)   1972-73, 1982-83
Arnie Whitaker (Blackburn)   1901-02, 1903-04

2

Eric Houghton (Aston Villa)	1931-32, 1933-34
Harry Davis (Sheff Wed)	1905-06 (h – FAC), 1905-06 (a)
Ivor Allchurch (Swansea)	1951-52 (2)
Jerry Dean (Notts County)	1905-06, 1910-11
Jock Hutton (Blackburn)	1928-29, 1931-32
Mick Channon (Southampton)	1979-80, 1980-81
Reg Mountford (Huddersfield)	1935-36, 1936-37
Tom Browell (Manchester City)	1919-20, 1922-23

Strangely, Charlie Buchan is the all-time leading scorer against Everton, with 19 goals in all competitions. He missed all three of his spot-kicks against the Toffees, remarkably all being saved by the Everton keeper, Tom Fern.

Other unexpected visitors

Yorkshire Terrier, Sheffield United (a), 12th September 1903

Straight after half-time a terrier got onto the playing area, 'causing much amusement' according to the *Daily Post*. The animal ran between the players, causing play to stop, and after being chased by several players from both sides the dog was eventually 'seized by the collar' by Archie Needham of the home team and escorted from the pitch.

One-legged man, Manchester United (h), 27th August 1921

Even Bobby Irvine's hat-trick could not overshadow arguably Goodison's greatest-ever gatecrasher. Deep into the second half, with Everton leading comfortably, a one-legged man without crutches invaded the playing area and proceeded, amongst much hilarity, to kick the ball from the touchline near the centre-circle back to the keeper.

Dog (breed unknown), Huddersfield (a), 23 April 1949

Then-record signing Aubrey Powell had little to cheer about in his time at Goodison. The forward was signed from Leeds for £20,000 in 1948 and his stay produced just five goals in 35 league matches. It did however produce one memorable incident, at Huddersfield at the tail – no pun intended - end of his first season. During the second half of the match a dog invaded the pitch and 'caused some amusement' according to the press before Powell grabbed hold of the canine interloper – a bit of a struggle followed which ended up with our friend biting the forward, before scampering from the pitch. Powell for some reason was allowed to stay on the playing area.

Jack Russell, West Brom (a), 27th November 1976

The visitor had such a profound influence on the game, he deserves his own feature – see Match 37.

The other worst penalty taken at Goodison

This has to be in the traditional Blues versus Whites public practise match, the annual pre-season friendly which used to take place between the first team and reserves, which took place in September 1930. Lachie McPherson kicked the ground instead of the ball when taking a penalty for the Whites, with the ball trickling very slowly into the hands of the keeper.

Ivor Allchurch (above left) - Missed a penalty at home, and away against Everton for Swansea; Cyril Lello (above right) on the treatment table, has scored at both ends on two occasions in an Everton shirt

THE GAMES

Left: Advertising cuttings taken from the 1897 FA Cup final programme, Everton v Aston Villa.

Below: Liverpool Daily Post & Echo coverage of the 1926 FA Cup ties between the Blues and Fulham.

FULHAM SURPRISE EVERTON.

BEECHAM'S GREAT SAVE IN LAST SECOND.

FULHAM BEAT EVERTON.

BEECHAM CARRIED OFF IN TRIUMPH

DEFEATED SIDE'S MERIT.

Above: 'Scrine, the Swansea inside-right, puts in a strong shot at Goodison Park before Lello and Jones get within challenging distance, but O'Neill was there to save.' Action from Everton v Swansea Town, 1952

Above: Bobby Collins helps give Johnny Carey a rousing send-off by netting No 2 from the penalty spot against Cardiff City, April 1961

This page: Everton v Southampton, 1971. Above: David Johnson strikes. Middle and below: Four-goal Joe Royle wreaks havoc

Opposite page: Everton v Leeds United, 1964. Brian Labone and Bobby Collins traipse off the Goodison turf to 'cool down',

Crystal Palace v Everton, 1972. Above: Five of the Blues' youngsters prepare to set off for their FA Cup blooding in the capital - from left: Mick Lyons, Gary Jones, Terry Darracott, Peter Scott, John McLaughlin

Above: Two fans rush onto the Selhurst Park pitch as the tie threatens to boil over. Palace goalkeeper Jackson grabs one of the 'invaders'.
Below: Alan Whittle becomes the latest player to enter referee Tommy Dawes' notebook

Above: Alan Whittle's initial shot hits the bar, while (below) Whittle fires Everton's first on the rebound

Below: Colin Harvey's strike crashes through the Palace defence to earn a Goodison Park replay. 'Everton survive Selhurst savagery' hailed the original cutting

Norwich City v Everton, 1973. Above: Dave Clements' effort finds its way in via a deflection off Duncan Forbes for the Blues' first goal

Above: Mike Bernard's shot finds the target via the foot of Dave Stringer, with celebrations to follow (below and opposite top)

Above: Goal No 3, as Mick Buckley's cross is headed into his own net by Duncan Forbes, his second of the afternoon past his own keeper. Left: If looks could kill...Forbes (No 5) and Norwich City goalkeeper Kevin Keelan exchange pleasantries

Everton v Manchester United, 1975. Above: A stunned Dai Davies contemplates Lou Macari's opener, 'a spectacular back kick', the Scot having just given the visitors a one-goal lead

Above: Bob Latchford levels before the break past Alex Stepney, and wheels away in celebration (below)

Finn Harps v Everton, 1978. Left: Bob Latchford in aerial action, with some 'subdued' local supporters looking on from the fencing... Everton v Finn Harps, 1978. Below: Andy King curls home the opener at Goodison

Watford v Everton, 1984. Above: Graeme Sharp reignites Everton hopes with the third goal

Above: The comeback is complete, as Adrian Heath fires home from the edge of the area, and (below) Heath sets off in celebration

Chelsea v Everton, 1985. Above: Graeme Sharp misses the target from the penalty spot. Below: Neville Southall has lost his shirt to skipper Kevin Ratcliffe, after being sent off

Everton v Southampton, 1986. Above: Derek Mountfield opens the scoring with what looks suspiciously like a hand

Above: Two different shots of Gary Lineker's first goal, a chip over the stranded Keith Grainger. Below: Lineker's second, Everton's fourth with only 36 minutes gone

Everton v Watford, 1986. Top: A goalmouth scramble following Neil Adams' cross-shot.
Middle: Derek Mountfield finds the net at the right end to stun the Hornets.
Left: Watford goalkeeper Steve Sherwood looks on anxiously as Adrian Heath goes close

Everton v Wimbledon, 1994. Above: The message is clear ahead of the game. Below: Graham Stuart holds his nerve from the spot to pull a goal back before half-time

Below: Barry Horne's speculative half volley finds the top corner and the comeback is nearly complete

Left: Two-goal hero Graham Stuart tries to avoid these Evertonians at the end of the Everton v Wimbledon match, 1994

Everton v Blackburn Rovers, 2006.
Below: David Weir's appeals prove in vain, as Iain Turner is sent off.

'Babes' rocked

Shock result at Old Trafford
Manchester United 2-5 Everton
First Division, 20th October, 1956

'On the face of it, the Goodison Park team is in for a heavy beating…their football in the past two games has been lamentable. If Everton could pull out a draw that would be a feather in the cap, but even that looks out of the question.'

So said the *Liverpool Echo* on the eve of the Blues' visit to Old Trafford over 50 years ago. The evidence to support that judgment was conclusive: 19th place in the table with eight points from 13 matches, and coming off the back of a 3-0 home thrashing by Chelsea. Their opponents were reigning First Division champions, unbeaten in 26 league matches and had accrued 22 points out of a possible 24 since the start of the season. In the ranks they had Roger Byrne, Eddie Colman, Liam (Billy) Whelan, Tommy Taylor, Mark Jones, David Pegg and the incomparable Duncan Edwards, who had first risen to prominence in scoring an FA Youth Cup-winning goal against Everton three years before. All would perish at Munich 15 months later. Add in Bill Foulkes and a promising youngster called Bobby Charlton and the United team was nothing short of formidable.

Everton on the other hand were struggling. Four players were dropped from the side that had lost to Chelsea and there were recalls for veterans Peter Farrell and Tommy Eglington, with debuts for Jimmy Gauld – later identified as a ringleader in the 1960s bribe scandal – and, belatedly, Albert Dunlop, who had been a professional with the Toffees since 1949. The previous season Edwards had scored a rather fortuitous goal in the same fixture, when his header had hit the crossbar and bounced down clearly still in play, only to see the referee erroneously award a goal.

On the face of it the first 10 minutes went with expectations, Bobby Charlton scoring with a typical volley from a Pegg corner and matters were made worse by the enforced departure, through injury, of the Toffees' Ken Birch two minutes previous. But actually Everton should have been 2-0 up by that stage, with that combative forward George Kirby missing two great chances (it is worth mentioning that Kirby was reckoned by Jackie Charlton to be the toughest player he ever faced). What then followed was arguably the most remarkable victory in the club's history.

Despite being a man down the visitors dominated proceedings, with Kirby and Eglington both troubling Wood in the United goal, and to nobody's surprise Everton drew level after 17 minutes when Don Donovan moved up from right-back and shot powerfully past the United keeper, whose desperate attempts to punch the ball away only helped it into the net.

Everton continued to press hard for further goals as United now became slightly ragged, with their middle men allowing the home team no respite, although Dunlop's flying stop from Bobby Charlton's header was 'one of the most brilliant saves I have seen for a long time,' according to 'Stork' in the *Liverpool Echo*. Then Tony McNamara found space on the right, and his beautifully-flighted cross was met perfectly by Kirby, whose header passed under the despairing dive of Wood. That goal was on 38 minutes and just before half-time it was 3-1 as Gauld – whose stunning debut was made all the more remarkable as he had not trained for a week due to a heavy cold – charged powerfully through the middle and slipped the ball onto the in-running Eglington, who confidently chipped the ball into the net to shock the United faithful.

The Blues started the second half in the same manner in which they finished the first, by totally dominating the home side. McNamara tested Ray Wood in the United goal as did Birch – now back on the pitch – shortly afterwards. But then completely against the run of play United were back in the game, Barry's pass to Whelan let in the Irishman to score with some aplomb past Dunlop, although he looked suspiciously offside.

That goal changed the match completely, with United moving up a gear as they strove to preserve their unbeaten record. But they found debutant Albert Dunlop in heroic form in the away team's goal and he saved brilliantly from Taylor – shackled brilliantly throughout the game by T.E. Jones - and then Charlton. The Blues remained dangerous on the break and with Kirby leading the line magnificently they went 4-2 ahead midway through the second half, with a header by the powerful centre-forward from a McNamara cross following a brilliantly-worked move that involved both Fielding and Gauld.

Everton were now playing magnificently, making a complete ass of the formbook. According to the *Liverpool Echo*: 'Everyone of the 11 Everton players was on his toes. No United man was given any latitude, he had to fight for every ball he got.' Remarkably the Blues went all-out for a fifth goal, and they got their just rewards seconds from the end, when another brilliantly-conceived move saw McNamara, who had been involved in three goals already, chip the ball over the advancing Wood.

The referee blew for full time shortly afterwards and the stunned crowd gave Everton a standing ovation. United's 26-match unbeaten run was ended and so was an undefeated run at home that had lasted for 33 matches since April 1955. The last team to beat the Busby Babes at Old Trafford before this memorable game - Everton, of course.

POSTSCRIPT:

Matt Busby was fulsome in his praise of the underdogs: 'Everton were well worth their win. They played very, very well.' Veteran reporter Stork in the *Liverpool Echo* proclaimed it the best Everton victory he had seen since the famous 6-4 win over Sunderland at Goodison in 1935.

The national press was equally amazed at the events at Old Trafford, with the *Daily Telegraph* reporting: 'Spectators at grounds all over the country rubbed their eyes and looked again when the half-time score went up and again at full time as United slipped to a humiliating defeat.'

What did the *Manchester Evening News* have to say about the game? Surprisingly they were complimentary about the away side: 'Well for once a team came up with a good answer to the United magic. Everton allowed them no room to work in. Close marking, fast covering in defence and the razor-sharp attack of United was blunted. Also Byrne and Foulkes never had the mastery over the Everton attack.'

This judgement rubber-stamps what remains arguably the most inspiring (and unexpected) victory in the club's history – when people say Everton's best-ever performance is a match against United in October when five goals were scored, perhaps they should be talking about this game instead!

Everton would beat Arsenal 4-0 at Goodison the following Saturday – what price nine goals in consecutive matches against United and Arsenal these days – but an inconsistent spell would follow and the side eventually finished 15th. United successfully defended their crown. A visit to Old Trafford in the FA Cup in February saw the Toffees slip to a 1-0 defeat with

Edwards netting the winner.

There was another curiosity about Everton visits to United in that season. Both the reserve and youth teams went there in the same week early in 1957 and again the matches ended 5-2 – this time to United.

Everton's first goal from Donovan, misjudged by United goalkeeper Wood

Kirby heads home from McNamara's cross

Five disallowed goals

Dave hunted by Wolves
Everton 1-0 Wolverhampton Wanderers
First Division, 24th August, 1957

D ave Hickson's return to the club in 1957 was in a bad-tempered
game, both on and off the pitch, that also had tragic consequences.
Crowd unrest and misconduct from the participants meant that this
contest, in many ways, was a forerunner of the more publicised encounter
against Leeds at Goodison seven years later.

The first match of the season is always eagerly anticipated, but the
opening fixture of the 1957-58 campaign was especially so, as the
magnificently-coiffured forward was back in town after a nomadic two-year
spell away. Mick Meagan was also in the starting line-up for the first time,
against a Wolves side that were in their pomp under the shrewd stewardship
of Stan Cullis.

Wolves were out of the blocks quickly, and in the opening minute Don
Donovan had to move quickly to shoulder Jimmy Mullen off the ball as he
moved menacingly towards the Everton goal. Two minutes later and the ball
was in the net for the first time, although it was disallowed for offside
against both Derek Temple and the diminutive winger, Graham Williams.
Remarkably it was to be the first of five disallowed goals.

Wolves bossed the first half until an unsavoury incident, in which typically
big Dave was cast as the villain, when he was innocent in most spectators'
eyes. A long cross from Jimmy Harris was met by both Hickson and the
Wolves keeper, Mal Finlayson, simultaneously. As we know that Dave never
knowingly came out second-best in such encounters, Finlayson went down
injured and required treatment for several minutes.

Hickson was just as much sinned against as a sinner during his Everton
career, and afterwards he came in for some harsh treatment, being badly
fouled by Eddie Clamp and blatantly sent sprawling into the cinder track at
pitch-side by Billy Wright. At that point bottles came onto the pitch at the
Park End, which had to be cleared by photographers, and moments later

referee Black had to visit the Gwladys Street End to confront a fan. Police also patrolled the dead-ball line at the Wolves end on foot (coincidentally the programme that day had a warning to spectators over behaviour, following an incident in a Central League game at Goodison in April).

Shortly afterwards Everton had the ball in the net for a second time when Meagan headed home, but the referee ruled for offside. The home side were back in the game and Temple came close to netting the opener but he was stopped by a fine diving save at his feet by Finlayson. Then just before half-time came a third disallowed goal for the home team, this time only the referee recognised an infringement for offside when Temple curled a brilliantly-executed shot past Finlayson. Such a poor decision did nothing to placate the already inflamed crowd.

The Wolves' team were greeted with boos as they entered the field on the resumption. The away team pressed immediately and this time it was their turn to feel a sense of injustice, when Jimmy Murray's header from 12 yards was disallowed, for reasons that were not apparent. That made it four disallowed goals inside 52 minutes.

As Wright tracked Hickson around the pitch, the Wolves player was continually vilified by the fans, with the forward showing his frustration at the referee by theatrically throwing himself into the penalty area after one particularly crude challenge - even though the offence was clearly several yards outside. The home side got a reward nevertheless on 70 minutes when Jimmy Harris fired home from 20 yards after some typically inventive work by Temple.

But the game would not have been complete without another contentious offside decision, Everton being denied for a fourth time when Hickson netted – it was that sort of day for him.

POSTSCRIPT:

This game is included because not only did it feature five disallowed goals (the most in an Everton game) but it also acted as a template for many games in the decades that followed, when a combination of poor player behaviour and inconsistent refereeing on the pitch led to unrest off it. There was also an appallingly tragic aspect to the day, when two spectators – one from Walton, and a Wolves fan from Stafford – collapsed and died as a result of shock, due to the excitement of the game.

In 2006 a national newspaper asked readers to nominate the match they had seen that had featured the most disallowed goals. Four was the best anyone could come up with – so did this match feature more than any game played in this country?

One of Derek Temple's many efforts on goal, saved by Finlayson. The original caption noted: 'He hits 'em hard and true for a man not long in senior football. I think he has a big future as an inside-forward'

The final act - the fifth and final goal disallowed, with Dave Hickson unlucky on this occasion

Nightmare at ToTENham

Blues set unwanted record
Tottenham Hotspur 10-4 Everton
First Division, 11th October, 1958

This game has a permanent place in the Everton Hall of Shame. But although the score tells a story, it doesn't tell the full tale, as the statistics show that if the Toffees had converted their chances at the same ratio as the home side, then a final score of, say, 10-7 would have been more realistic. As it was several unwanted club records were set, most notably the most number of goals conceded by the Blues in a first-team game. There was also the famous case of Jimmy Harris netting a hat-trick and still being on the losing side. He was not the first Everton player to achieve this feat though, that fell to John Bell who scored all three of the goals in a 4-3 loss at Aston Villa in September 1895. It is also worth mentioning that no away team scored more goals than Everton that day although the fact that Spurs scored six more goals than anyone else is of greater relevance!

The match is of course also memorable for Tottenham fans. Bill Nicholson, who was to become their most successful and revered manager, was famously appointed on the morning of the game although the players were not informed until 15 minutes before kick-off. Nicholson, as a former player and then first-team coach, was the natural replacement for Jimmy Anderson. He had resigned due to ill-health after a 50-year association with the club, primarily as a result of the pressures of trying to live up to the standards of his predecessor Arthur Rowe, the man who had led Spurs to their first-ever league title in 1951.

That was also the year of Nicholson's only England appearance, at Goodison Park of all places, where he scored with his first touch after 19 seconds and was never selected again, his chances being restricted by the presence of Billy Wright. After Nicholson retired he quickly gained a reputation as an innovative coach and he served in that capacity for England in the 1958 World Cup finals. The new manager had also unwittingly already played a part in shaping the future of Everton, turning down the chance to manage Sheffield Wednesday, giving the opportunity for Harry Catterick to show the managerial potential that would eventually result in a return to Goodison Park.

Nicholson was also a typical example of a general rule about football managers: they will often produce sides whose style of play is the polar opposite of their own. Nicholson was a dour Yorkshireman and pragmatic half-back, whose teams – especially the 1961 Double side – played with a flair and elegance that has been rarely matched in the post-War era. That was in contrast to, say, his contemporary Don Revie, who was an expansive and progressive forward, but as a manager produced teams that often operated outside the boundaries of fair play, as Everton would find out on more than one occasion over the next decade. Nicholson did have his moments and it was he, rather than Bill Shankly, who first uttered the phrase: 'If a player is not interfering with play – what is he doing on the pitch?'

The Spurs team that day, the last to be selected by Anderson, contained only two players – the ball-playing genius that was Danny Blanchflower and that fine centre-forward Bobby Smith – who would clinch the Double at Wembley in 1961. At outside-right was an intriguing player, Tommy Harmer, who possessed just as much skill as Blanchflower but had difficultly harnessing that talent within the team's pattern of play. Consequently Harmer tended to have bad days and good days – and none went better than the visit of Everton in October 1958. Also in the Spurs team was another fine midfielder, Jim Iley, who has three claims to fame involving the Blues. The first is this game; the second was his penalty following Gordon West's notorious sending off at St James' Park in 1967 (see Match 50) and finally, all Evertonians can be grateful that as manager of Bury he gave Neville Southall his league debut and then agreed to sell the great man to the Toffees.

Everton were also experiencing problems. After setting one unwanted club record of the worst start to a season ever (six straight defeats) they had sacked manager Ian Buchan. Team selection was now in the hands of the directors, prior to the arrival of Johnny Carey, which was to be two weeks later. The Blues had recovered with four wins out of five going into the clash, although the line-up was a cause for concern, especially a back-line that featured two inexperienced full-backs in John Bramwell and Alan

Sanders with a young Johnny King also in the line-up.

The Toffees also featured Brian and Jimmy Harris, Bobby Collins, Dave Hickson and Wally Fielding (who would never play for the club again after playing 410 games, scoring 54 goals in the process). The keeper was Albert Dunlop, who had replaced the injured Jimmy O'Neill in the midweek friendly against South Africa, and had promptly conceded four goals in 40 minutes.

According to contemporary press reports, on hearing in the dressing room that Nicholson had been appointed, Spurs promised to a man that they would mark the occasion by doing their best with a convincing victory. Unfortunately for the visitors, they were true to their word.

The die was cast as early as the third minute, when Brian Harris lost his footing in midfield, enabling Bobby Smith to fire in a shot that was deflected into the path of Alf Stokes, who finished with ease. Little did the 37,000 crowd know that there would be another 13 goals in the game. Everton could have equalized immediately, with both Hickson and Collins bringing fine saves from Hollowbread in the Tottenham goal. They did draw level though when Hickson outpaced John Ryden on the Spurs right and his cross-shot was put in by Jimmy Harris from five yards out. But within four minutes the home side were back in front. Harmer had now moved to the left and his cross was met perfectly by Smith, whose header left Dunlop with no chance.

Spurs were now firmly in the ascendancy and not for the first time a side had raised their game following the appointment of a new manager, with Blanchflower and Harmer in particular running riot, the latter's free-kick falling straight to Smith who shot straight at Dunlop. The Toffees were having 'a tough time of it' according to the *Liverpool Echo* and George Robb was allowed to shoot unchallenged through three Everton defenders to make it 3-1 after half-an-hour. A minute later it was four, Blanchflower moving down the right, and Smith converted his low cross.

The Toffees remarkably were still creating enough chances to stay in the game, and Jimmy Harris and Collins were both guilty of wasting opportunities from 10 yards out. But Spurs' movement and pace were causing all sorts of problems and on 34 minutes Stokes made it 5-1, after George Robb's header had been parried by Dunlop. It was no surprise that two minutes before the break it was six, with Terry Medwin scoring with a fine shot that cannoned in off the post.

Everton continued to make a fist of it in the second half, with the score not really reflecting their efforts, the *Daily Express* pointing out that 'although they were outclassed, they were by no means disgraced.' They were rewarded when Jimmy Harris headed in from Fielding's corner. But just after the hour Robb's shot was allowed to cross the face of goal and Smith twisted to score from an acute angle to complete his hat-trick. The score now stood at 7-2.

The game now entered a fallow period for goals, as the encounter acquired a niggly edge, with a clash between Johnny King and Ryden leading to heated exchanges between the players. To their credit the Toffees continued to battle hard and they blocked out the rampant home team until eight minutes from time when Dunlop's poor clearance was struck perfectly back into the net by Harmer from just outside the box.

On 83 minutes the score was appropriately 8-3 when Jimmy Harris completed his own hat-trick from a Dave Hickson centre. Bobby Smith then missed the chance of the game, shooting high into the stand from just three yards out. Two minutes later the home team scored another when Stokes' centre was nodded past Dunlop by Smith for his fourth. For the first time ever Everton had conceded nine goals in a first-team game.

The Blues still showed plenty of fight and three minutes from time they got a further reward when Collins' speculative shot flew straight past Hollowbread. But astonishingly the scoring was still not over, Spurs having the final word when Harmer's free-kick from the right was headed in by Ryden.

POSTSCRIPT:

The *Daily Telegraph* was gushing in its praise of the home side: 'It was true to suggest that the best defence in England would have been crushed at White Hart Lane this afternoon.' The first half of the newspaper's next remark about one Everton player might surprise those with long memories: 'Dave Hickson, apart from being a model of the sort of behaviour the FA is calling for, is developing into a very good centre-forward.'

Despite having conceded 14 goals in just over two hours of football, Albert Dunlop was in jovial mood after the game: 'I thought Spurs were a bit unlucky, and my back is aching a bit having bent over to pick the ball up from the net so often.'

Most goals conceded by Everton

10
Tottenham Hotspur   10-4   Everton   11th October 1958

8
Huddersfield Town   8-2   Everton   7th April 1953
Newcastle United   8-2   Everton   7th November 1959

The Huddersfield match featured an interesting curiosity in that Jimmy Glazzard scored four goals for the home side, all from headers, with all the crosses coming from their left-winger Vic Metcalf. Glazzard joined Everton three years later, but was offloaded after just three months and three games with no goals.

On 7th March 1942 a strong Everton team – featuring Joe Mercer, Tommy Lawton and Alex Stevenson – visited Molineux for a Wartime League match against Wolves. They returned home having been thrashed 11-1, the heaviest defeat ever inflicted on an Everton side in any match. Jack Rowley scored five times and Frank Broome netted a hat-trick.

Highest goals aggregate in a league match

17
Tranmere Rovers   13-4   Oldham A. (Div 3 N) 26th December 1935

14
Aston Villa   12-2   Accrington S. (Div 1) 12th March 1892
Tottenham Hotspur   10-4   Everton (Div 1)   11th October 1958

A Harris hat-trick

At the tail-end of the 1955-56 season, for the only time in their league history, Everton had three players in their line-up with the same surname: Albert, Jimmy and Brian Harris playing in three matches. They were unrelated.

Both Jimmy and Brian featured in the 10-4 match at Spurs, which remains a unique result in English football. Since that day there has only been one, new and still unique result in a league match. That occurred on Boxing Day 1962, when for the first time ever a score of 11-0 was recorded as Oldham thrashed Southport. The unlucky goalkeeper that day was none other than the third member of the triumvirate from Everton - Albert Harris!

Tottenham managers obviously like to play Everton in their first match in charge of the North London club, for not only was Bill Nicholson successful, but in August 1984 Peter Shreeves won his first match in charge 4-1 at Goodison and 13 years later Christian Gross won 1-0 at the same venue.

Above, top left: Blues keeper Jimmy O'Neill is challenged by Huddersfield's Cavanagh and Glazzard, while (above right) Jimmy Glazzard scores the first of his four headers against the Blues in his side's 8-2 romp at Leeds Road, April 1953. Above, left: Brian Harris, on target against Nottingham Forest, with namesake Jimmy closing in second right

Blues score eight at Anfield!

13-goal Cup final
Everton 8-5 Tranmere Rovers
Liverpool Senior Cup final, 11th May, 1959

Although recent years have not been so fertile, Everton have won more league games at Anfield against Liverpool than any other club. Their best result in that time was 5-0, achieved in October 1914. But their largest haul at the home of their rivals, since they left for Goodison in 1892, was saved for a Liverpool Senior Cup final against their other neighbours, from across the Mersey, over 40 years ago.

In those days, due to temporary separation of the city's big two from 1951-62, the Senior Cup held an attraction far greater than it does today. Some of the most memorable moments in Mersey soccer were during this period, including the first floodlit matches at Goodison and Anfield in 1957.

The league campaign had just finished and the Blues had finished 16th in the First Division whilst Tranmere had ended a long campaign 7th in Division Three. Such was the importance of the cup in those halcyon days that Everton fielded a full-strength team, whilst Rovers lined up with former Goodison stalwarts Peter Farrell and Tommy Eglington. Ironically Everton had visited Anfield the previous week and had lost 1-0 to Liverpool in a Lancashire Senior Cup semi-final.

The crowd of just over 14,000 saw a quite astonishing match, best summarized by simply listing the goals in chronological order:

1-0   In a fantastic first half the Blues opened the scoring as quickly as the fourth minute, when an unmarked Bobby Laverick shot fiercely past unsighted Rovers keeper George Payne.

2-0   Three minutes later Laverick doubled his tally, turning in from close range after Payne had failed to hold a Jimmy Harris cross.

2-1   After 26 minutes Rovers halved the deficit, when Farrell was adjudged to have been brought down in the area, and it was his former Toffees team-mate Eglington who shot home confidently from the spot.

3-1   Remarkably, the two-goal margin was restored within 60 seconds, when a mistake by David Frith let Eddie Thomas in on goal, the Blues forward slipping the ball easily past Payne.

3-2   Just after the half-hour mark Rovers got themselves back into the contest when Keith Williams headed in from a perfectly-crafted Eglington centre.

3-3   Within 60 seconds this encounter took another twist when Williams headed in again from another Eglington cross. Immediately from the kick-off, Williams almost produced a miraculous hat-trick, but his 50-yard run was halted in front of goal.

4-3   Six minutes before half-time Everton went ahead again when centre-forward Frank Wignall scored with a fine shot on the turn.

5-3   The crowd had barely had the time to finish the half-time cuppa when in the 48th minute Eddie Thomas became the third player to record two goals on the night, shooting strongly past the Rovers keeper.

6-3   Within three minutes Dave Hickson, who had been in a rampaging mood after being given far too much space by the Rovers defence, sent the Blues clear with a great header past Payne.

7-3   In the 54th minute, remarkably Hickson added to his total with a fine goal after being put through on goal. Ten goals within the first hour!

The floodlights were then switched on midway through the second half, which pre-empted a relative drought in the scoring, with Tranmere failing to trouble the Everton keeper Dunlop whilst at the other end only two fine saves by Payne stopped the Blues surging further ahead. But this lull was only temporary:

8-3   Up until the 77th minute only Jimmy Harris of the Everton forwards had failed to find the Tranmere net, but he made amends with a fine shot past Payne.

8-4   Tranmere were not finished though. Keith Williams had proved a handful for the Everton defence all night, and after 81 minutes he completed a well-deserved hat-trick with a fine shot on the turn.

8-5   Tommy Eglington had been Rovers' best player with Williams and three minutes later the Irishman completed the scoring with the final goal of the evening.

Thus concluded the entertainment for a disbelieving crowd, which surely kept them happy throughout the close season. It was a night when 13 was a lucky number for everyone.

POSTSCRIPT:

Everton beat Tranmere again in the final the following season 5-2. It was Peter Farrell's final game as a player, appropriately against the club he had served with so much distinction.

Eddie Thomas (left) and Tommy Eglington (above) - both were involved in the 1959 Liverpool Senior Cup final

Carey's farewell
Jeers and cheers
Everton 5-1 Cardiff City
First Division, 15th April, 1961

The sacking of Johnny Carey has quite rightly entered Merseyside soccer folklore. Most people are now familiar with the tale that on 14th April 1961, when he and the Everton chairman John Moores were in a taxi whilst attending a meeting of league chairmen in London, Mr Moores informed the former Irish international that he was sacked as manager. Carey had been in the post for two-and-a-half years.

The background to the dismissal can be traced to Moores joining the board at Goodison in the 1959-60 season and his ascent to the chairmanship the following summer. Although the team had started the campaign well – by the beginning of December 1960 they stood second, which was the club's highest league placing since the War – a slump after Christmas of eight defeats in nine matches had left Carey vulnerable. It was in this period that the Board voted unanimously for him to be relieved of his post.

Apart from results, the other aspect of the situation was the alleged clash of personalities between the manager and chairman: Carey's methods of arm-round-the-shoulder when dealing with players did not curry favour with the more aggressive, regimented approach demanded by Moores, who had of course invested heavily into the club (indeed, in early 1961 Moores spoke directly to the players and criticized them in Carey's presence, something that clearly undermined the manager and also upset Bobby Collins, who was singled out for personal criticism).

Ironically by the time of the fateful visit to the capital, the crisis had been averted and a 4-0 win at Newcastle the previous Saturday had been the third victory in four matches, with the other drawn. Alex Young had returned from injury and the first seeds of his fruitful partnership with Roy Vernon had been sown, whilst relative newcomers like Billy Bingham, George Thomson and Jimmy Gabriel were now settled in.

On the day after he was effectively sacked, Everton were due to play Cardiff

City in their penultimate home match of the season. Carey remained in the post for the game and consequently both the build-up, and the match itself, was enveloped by the slightly surreal atmosphere generated by the twitchy crowd. From quite early on it was clear that the eyes of the spectators would be focused on the front row of the directors' box and not the players.

When John Moores appeared first, it was apparent with whom the crowd sympathized – the Everton chairman was roundly booed by almost everyone present and that was followed by slow handclapping and chants of 'We want Carey!' When the manager (or ex-manager) appeared he was greeted with cheers and he then sat, diplomatically, in the second row of the directors' box behind his chairman.

The match itself provided a fitting send-off for the manager. The home side attacked with vigour from the start, and had the ball in the net as early as the first minute but Bingham, who had headed home, was deemed to be offside. Nevertheless the home crowd did not have long to wait for the first goal as, on four minutes, a brilliant move commenced with a fine cross-field ball by Labone to Collins, who exchanged passes with Young and shot powerfully past Maurice Swan.

The home side continued to dominate after the opener with Young's play, particularly, catching the eye although the former Hearts player should have done better when he shot over from just five yards after a speedy move involving Bingham and Vernon. Just before the half-hour mark, after two unrewarded penalty appeals, Vernon raced into the area only to be felled by Harrington – the referee immediately pointing to the spot and Collins confidently netted for his second of the afternoon.

The crowd lapped up the performance; it was easily the best of the season and they wasted no time in expressing their support for Carey, who must have watched with some bemusement. Just before the break the Toffees went 3-0 up, another scintillating move that began with a 30-yard run by Collins, finished with Vernon teeing up Young with such precision that the Everton forward did not have to break stride before rounding the keeper and scoring the fourth league goal of his Goodison career.

The second half began in peculiar fashion, John Moores took his seat in the directors' box to the jeers of the crowd and, whilst their attention was focused on the Main Stand, Young scored his second of the day when a loose ball fell kindly into his path. It was timed at 10 seconds after the restart, and barely anyone in the ground had noticed.

Three minutes later the Everton scoring for the afternoon was complete when team captain Collins headed home a hard-driven cross by Bingham to complete his own hat-trick. Shortly afterwards the Cardiff keeper, Swan, was injured, suffering a broken collar-bone and was replaced by the centre-forward Derek Tapscott. Strangely this had a negative effect on the home side, who became slightly sluggish as a result of their overpowering dominance against 10 men. Tapscott also proved to be a more than capable replacement, with one save from Vernon being worthy of the man he replaced. Seven minutes from time Cardiff ventured into the Everton penalty area and Dai Ward coolly slotted home a consolation goal, which was richly deserved for the fighting qualities they had displayed against a sparkling home team.

POSTSCRIPT:

England's 9-3 rout of Scotland at Wembley was the biggest football story of the day, but John Carey's last match as manager was one to remember and he was cheered both after the match and in the car park afterwards. After leaving the Goodison hot-seat Carey joined Leyton Orient and guided them into Division One in his first season.

Although the Londoners were relegated in the Blues' title-winning campaign of 1962-63, he at least gained satisfaction in a 3-0 win over Everton at Brisbane Road. Carey subsequently took charge of Nottingham Forest, and was manager when they defeated the Toffees 3-2 in a wonderful FA Cup quarter-final at the City Ground in 1967.

After sacking Carey, John Moores was then left with the enviable task of finding a replacement that met his requirements. That was easy though, newly available on the market was a manager who had a reputation for being both a ruthless disciplinarian and an uncompromising taskmaster, as well as being a former Everton player to boot - his name was Harry Catterick.

Far left: Johnny Carey, hailed by the Everton fans in his last game in charge, a 5-1 demolition of Cardiff City which saw Bobby Collins (left) notch a hat-trick

Freak game at Goodison

Ref and keeper carried off
Everton 4-2 Aston Villa
First Division, 28th February, 1964

‘ The most freakish, most eventful game ever played at Goodison,’ said
Michael Charters of the *Liverpool Echo* - and he'd seen a few. Six goals,
one penalty, two referees, four linesmen (one the Everton coach), a keeper
carried off, three bookings and three open goals missed by the home team.
Add in a second half that was almost invisible to spectators, and this Friday
night fixture was one to remember for a 50,000 crowd.

Everton really should have retained the title in the 1963-64 season, but a loss
of form in the run-in – coupled with the *Sunday People's* infamous exposé of
alleged match-fixing that implicated Tony Kay, amongst others - meant that
the championship, that was theirs for the taking, slipped across Stanley Park.

When Aston Villa visited at the end of February, the Blues stood third in the
table, four points behind Spurs and a point below Liverpool. The Midlands'
side were managed by Joe Mercer, a man for whom the word 'genial' could
only have been conceived. The former Everton great enjoyed a successful
managerial career, but Villa in the mid-1960s were very much on the slippery
slope – one that would lead improbably to Third Division football in the early
1970s. (Joe seemed a natural to be Goodison boss, but unfortunately for both
parties it was never to be. It has rarely been mentioned that he was offered the
post in 1956 but, being the gentleman he was, the great man turned it down on
account of his contract with Sheffield United. The Board went for Ian Buchan,
a choice that baffles to this day.)

The game took place on a Friday night on account of our rivals across the
Park playing Swansea in the FA Cup at Anfield the next day (there were no
Sunday matches in those days, of course). Everton lined up at full strength
whilst one name in the Villa line-up caught the eye at right-back – Gordon
Lee.

Villa went ahead after five minutes, when good build-up play by Deakin and
Phil Woosnam – later to be a major player in the development of football in

the USA – left Harry Burrows with an easy chance to score.

Although Everton pressed hard, the Villa defence held firm – the only incident of note in the Villa area being a collision between Geoff Sidebottom, the visiting keeper and Alex Young on the half-hour, during which the Villa player received an accidental blow to the face. One other aspect of the game was a running battle between Villa's Ron Wylie and the combative and ultra-competitive Tony Kay – at one point a strong challenge by the midfielder resulted in his boot completely ripping open the shirt of the Villa forward, which led to the referee checking Kay's boots to ensure they possessed studs, not razor blades.

Almost immediately the referee, Mr Bill Hollan, had his own health to worry about when a collision with an Everton player led him to fall awkwardly and twist a knee in the process. As ambulance-men and players surrounded the stricken match official, the Villa keeper Sidebottom fell face-first into the mud in the Villa penalty box. All his team-mates, rather bizarrely, ran across the pitch from one injured party to another, and it was soon apparent that the keeper was suffering from delayed-action concussion. This also meant that Villa were down to 10 men, with the centre-half John Sleeuwenhoek (who despite the name was an England U23 international) taking over between the posts.

As there was no such thing as a fourth official then, a volunteer linesman was required quickly, so step forward from the Everton bench, Ron Lewin, the first-team coach! As ludicrous as it may seem, there was no rule to prevent such an eventuality, in fact he had performed the same role against West Brom three years before. After a delay of seven minutes, the action restarted and typically Lewin's neutrality was tested almost immediately. A cross from Vernon saw Young head the ball back for Dennis Stevens to throw himself at the ball and force it over the line. But the Villa players surrounded the new referee, Mr H. Burns, on the basis that:

a) Young was clearly offside; and:

b) the official who made (or did not make) the decision was his coach - although not unreasonable points, the referee rebuffed their complaints and ran swiftly to the centre-circle.

At this juncture, the police were forced into the crowd in front of the Main Stand to arrest several of the crowd 'who had offended them by word or action' according to the *Liverpool Echo*. Also, quite sensibly, an appeal to the crowd was made for another official – to replace Lewin - to run the line, and down came Mr J.D. Jones (who came from Moreton, for the record). Not for the first and last time, the replacement referee was the target of some mischief from the players. First Wylie entered his book for aiming a kick at Kay, and then Sleeuwenhoek's kicking of the ball into the crowd in protest at the award of a free-kick led to him following suit. It was 1-1 at half-time.

It was just as well the opening period was so action-packed, for if it had all happened in the second half then nobody would have seen it. A thick mist descended upon Goodison Park, making the match almost impossible to view unless you were close to the pitch. What did happen was that on 55 minutes a penalty was awarded when Roy Vernon was felled in the area, and the Welsh international dusted himself down to convert the spot-kick.

Eleven minutes later Everton went 3-1 ahead when Young netted after fine approach play by Scott and Vernon. Twenty minutes from time it was 4-1, when Alex Scott broke through and although the deputy keeper saved his first shot, the winger regained possession and slid the ball home. There was just enough time left for the future Arsenal manager, George Graham to lob Gordon West to make the score respectable. Shortly after the referee blew up for full time, to end one of the most controversial and exciting matches seen on the ground for several years.

POSTSCRIPT:

Understandably there was no shortage of after-match comments, although Harry Catterick was typically economical with his thoughts: "It was too rough for my enjoyment." One man who was not short of a few words was Joe Mercer, who was unusually frank in his opinion on the choice of replacement lineman: "What made the position doubly unfortunate was that Lewin was set to give decisions in which his club's forwards were concerned…this is not the first time Mr Lewin has acted as linesman here when a referee has been incapacitated."

Villa consequently sent a strongly worded note to the Football League to that effect, but no official action was taken. Meanwhile Alex Young – involved in two of the game's controversial incidents – was adamant that injury to the Villa keeper was accidental: "I turned to volley...but the first time Geoff was anywhere near me was when my shin cracked against his chin." As for his contentious goal, he was equally assertive: "I came back onside by checking my stride as the move built up." But Villa thought otherwise.

Thankfully, after a night in Broadgreen Hospital, the Villa keeper was released the following day.

Jimmy Hill runs the line

Never one to shirk the limelight, the bearded pundit/chairman/manager famously came from the stands to run the line after the referee was injured in an Arsenal v Liverpool clash at Highbury in September 1972. But Jimmy Hill also did the same in a match at Goodison in December 1963 against Chelsea but, some would say thankfully, it was not the hirsute one-time *Match of the Day* presenter on this occasion, rather his namesake, the Everton reserve (on this day at least) and Northern Ireland international.

When the referee Mr Windle was knocked out accidentally following a collision with Frank Blunstone of Chelsea, up stepped Hill from the Everton bench as a replacement for Mr Morrissey who, remarkably in his first league game as an official, now found himself as the new referee.

The replacement ref made a bit of a mess of his promotion, giving Chelsea a corner when an Everton free-kick was more appropriate and refusing two nailed-on penalties for the home team. He also finished three minutes early after forgetting to add any time on for the stoppage due to his predecessor's accident. Apart from that he did okay!

Ref knocked out by player

The meaningless end-of-season visit to Huddersfield in April 1948 was brought to life by a fine hat-trick by Jock Dodds in an easy Everton victory, and also an unfortunate incident involving the referee. After Dodds had just netted his first goal, a fine cross by Higgins from the Everton right was headed perfectly into the path of Alex Stevenson by Dodds, only for an opposition defender to handle the ball. The referee, Mr Williams, pointed to the spot, but simultaneously a clearance from a defender struck the official and knocked him out. After a lengthy delay he resumed his duties and it was no surprise that Eddie Wainwright's kick was saved by the keeper.

Player knocked out by ref

James Broad was a dangerous centre-forward in the post-World War I period but, unfortunately, he failed to catch fire at Goodison. In April 1925 Broad became the only Everton player to have been knocked-out by a referee. During the home match against Birmingham, the Toffees were refused a penalty and as the official moved his arm swiftly to wave play on, his elbow caught Broad flush on the chin, rendering him unconscious. Broad was carried-off the pitch but he returned later on – the crowd though were not fully aware of what had happened, and Mr Kingscott was roundly booed for the rest of the game.

Mr Shaw's short stay

The dying embers of Gordon Lee's managerial reign in April 1981 witnessed a match against Middlesbrough at Goodison that saw the fastest substitute in Everton history – but it wasn't one of the players. Referee Mr Shaw collapsed within a minute of the start with a twisted knee and, despite 10 minutes of treatment from both physios, he could not continue. The players wandered aimlessly around the pitch in the meantime and on the resumption he was replaced by Mr Riley, one of his linesmen. The Everton referee's steward Harry Sheriff (a great name for someone in authority) took over on the line as the Blues won 4-1.

Jimmy Hill running the line at Highbury in 1972 (left) and fellow substitute linesman, the 'other' Jimmy Hill (right), lining up in Everton's team photograph ahead of the 1964-65 campaign

Cooling off
Ref takes players from pitch
Everton 0-1 Leeds United
First Division, 7th November, 1964

In the 1960s a new word entered the footballing lexicon: 'Professionalism.' What sounds like a complimentary term was in fact the complete opposite - it was a catch-all phrase to reflect the new, cynical side of the game. Professionalism was characterized by niggling, nasty fouls (often out of sight of the referee), harassment of officials, bullying of opponents and time-wasting. No single team embraced the new creed like Don Revie's Leeds United, hence the soubriquet 'Dirty Leeds.'

How and when the Yorkshire side earned this nickname is unknown, although some say, perhaps unfairly, that the arrival from Everton of Bobby Collins in early 1962 was the catalyst. Although there is no doubt that the teak-hard Glaswegian brought a steely, competitive presence to the side, there were other reasons for the poor standing of the club. But there were enough flashpoints during the decade to support the view that the nickname was deserved.

The insightful Johnny Giles summed up the climate of the times better than most: "You had to establish a reputation that would make people think twice about messing with you. It was a different game then, much more physical than it is today – vicious even – and people like myself and Bobby Collins were targets…you either took it or responded to it." Also, not in doubt, was that with players like Giles, Bremner and Collins in the team, Leeds United could also play a bit.

Everton were not exactly shrinking violets at this time either. Two months earlier a particularly fractious encounter at Old Trafford had resulted in the referee, Mr J.E. Carr, calling all 22 players into the centre of the pitch for a warning about their behaviour and to cool things down a bit. It was the first time the many present had seen this in a top-class game in England. 'The worst possible advertisement for professional sportsmanship ever seen,' was one paper's view the next day.

Memories of a ferocious clash between the sides in the FA Cup the season before were still fresh when the teams took the field at Goodison on the first Saturday in November. It was Remembrance Sunday the following day, but there was nothing peaceful about what followed next: one of the most notorious games in the history of organised football in this country, one described in the *Sunday People* as 'spine chilling.' United were without England centre-forward Alan Peacock, and in his place was Rod Belfitt, a player who holds an equally notorious place in Goodison folklore, for entirely different reasons! (Belfitt signed for Everton in 1972. He only knew about the move when, walking his dog the morning after playing for Ipswich at Goodison, he bumped into manager Bobby Robson, who told him to pack his bags as he was going to Everton.)

The referee was Ken Stokes, a man who had sent Tony Kay off exactly 12 months before against Blackburn at Goodison. That match also featured such mass scenes of crowd unrest that Everton were forced to erect barriers at Goodison, the first time an English club had used this strategy.

The tone was set in the opening seconds with a bad foul on Fred Pickering and then erupted completely when Sandy Brown and Giles both went for the same ball just outside the Everton penalty area and Brown, incensed by the Leeds player's challenge, complained about 'stud marks in the chest' before throwing a left hook at his opponent. Referee Stokes stopped play, took Brown's name and then sent him off. The game was just four minutes old (Brown's dismissal remains the quickest by an Everton player in a first-team match). Jack Rowe in Monday's *Daily Post* made the point that the referee, who intended to act tough at the start of the match as a deterrent, had actually made things worse.

The home crowd was understandably incensed by this perceived injustice and vented their fury by throwing missiles onto the pitch. After 14 minutes of Leeds pressure – when there was some football, in between the constant free-kicks – the away side took the lead when a perceptive free-kick by Collins left full-back Willie Bell with a free header at the far post. Roy Vernon and Billy Bremner were enjoying their own personal duel, and it was from a free-kick awarded against the Welshman that Collins struck a free-kick from fully 35 yards that Rankin could only punch out.

A few minutes later came the moment for which the game became infamous. Bell and Derek Temple seemingly collided at full speed as they both followed the flight of the ball - although it was clear to most people present that Bell had clearly fouled the Everton player. As they both lay prone on the pitch the Everton players surrounded the referee, demanding that Bell should be dismissed. At that point Mr Stokes walked straight to the dressing room, with the players behind him. Such an action was unprecedented in league football. On the pitch Bell lay concussed and it took several minutes for the defender to come round whilst ambulance-men put Temple onto a stretcher. All around there was chaos - spectators were running onto the pitch and debris rained on from the terraces.

It was not clear initially what was happening. Had the game been abandoned? Shortly afterwards a statement from the Everton secretary was read over the loudspeakers, indicating that play would restart in five minutes, although Stokes also pointed out that if the behaviour of the crowd (and players) did not improve he would halt proceedings completely. Stokes visited both dressing rooms to reinforce that view, saying that he would report both teams to the football authorities. Catterick took the opportunity to show him the marks on Brown's chest following his clash with Giles.

When the players returned after a break of 10 minutes to 'cool off', the pitch was covered in cushions and the game restarted amid 'jeers and catcalls.' Interestingly the referee had awarded a free-kick to Everton, so maybe there was some substance to the players' protests over the foul by Bell. There was then a second announcement that if objects continued to be thrown onto the pitch, the match would be abandoned. The point should be made that both teams were equally culpable – Everton actually committed more fouls than Leeds – and to reinforce that point just before half-time Rees was guilty of a horrendous challenge on Collins.

On the restart both Hunter and Vernon were guilty of some harsh tackling until Everton, for the first time, got a foothold in the game without really threatening the Leeds goal. Jackie Charlton in particular was putting in an impressive display. Some of the bad feeling had blown itself out in the second half, thankfully, and even the *Liverpool Echo* made the point that 'a remarkable spell followed of five minutes without a foul.'

The home side continued to press, without much conviction, and Temple wasted the best chance when he shot into the side netting. Leeds held on for their 1-0 victory, but there were certainly no winners on such an appalling day.

POSTSCRIPT:

As can be expected, subsequent match reports did not focus on the football. In fact Leslie Edwards, in the leading article in the following Monday's *Daily Post*, stated: '...followers of the game are debating what can be done to cure the disease of foul play on the pitch and foul behaviour on the terraces.' *The Times* blamed the crowd and the visitors: 'Goodison Park has already gained an unsavoury tribal reputation for vandalism. Leeds United have earned black marks for ill temper on the field. The marriage of these two dangerous elements sparked off the explosion.' Jack Rowe in the *Daily Post* was more explicit, pointing out that some of the violence could have been avoided if Stokes had (rightly) dismissed Bell for the foul on Temple.

Elsewhere the ball was firmly in the court of Joe Richards, the President of the Football League. "The time has come to investigate the whole question of these ugly scenes and rows. They are bringing a bad image to football," was his view. But Richards' power within the game had been diluted following his backing down against Jimmy Hill and the PFA over the maximum wage row in 1961. Which was just as well for the clubs: remarkably Leeds escaped punishment whilst Sandy Brown was suspended for two weeks and Everton were fined £250 for failure to control the crowd. Efforts to curb the violence within the game would require greater sanctions than that.

To end on an upbeat note, in August 1965 Richards proclaimed to the press: "Put your money this season on Liverpool to win the championship, Everton to win the FA Cup and England to win the World Cup." One wonders if he did?

To show how lucky Leeds were not to be charged with anything, three years later they were fined the princely sum of 10 guineas for arriving at Goodison for a league match without away socks, so there was a clash with Everton's. Ironically this rule had been brought in after the Toffees had gone to Stamford Bridge the season before with no alternative to their white socks, and had to wear Chelsea's yellow away stockings instead.

Toiletries disallow goal

Although it never rose to the 'heights' reached by the Everton v Leeds encounter, the visit to Maine Road in November 1966 was also bad tempered, and featured the best reason ever for disallowing a goal in any Blues match. After Jimmy Gabriel had hooked home Alex Scott's free-kick, hopes that Everton had equalized were dashed when the ref disallowed the goal...as he was picking up toilet rolls at the time. The match official claimed he did not signal the free-kick to be taken, being too busy removing the toiletries from the goalmouth. When the kick was retaken a mad scramble ensued with many players falling on top of the ball in the six-yard box: 'A mass of humanity pushing and pulling in front of the goal,' in the *Liverpool Echo's* words. The ref was forced to order a drop ball.

Everton lost 1-0 in a match that featured a vicious feud between City's Dave Connor and Alan Ball, which resulted in Harry Catterick ordering the fiery midfielder to play in attack to avoid his marker. (Three years later the Everton boss would make repeated attempts to bring Connor to Goodison from Maine Road. His introduction to Ball at Bellefield would have been interesting!)

Sandy Brown makes the lonely walk after being sent off against Leeds, with United boss Don Revie turning his attention elsewhere

The best reserve game ever

'Incredible decisions by the referee'
Newcastle reserves 2-3 Everton reserves
Central League, 3rd May, 1969

Type 'Bahrain' and 'penalty' into an internet search engine and you get all sorts of stuff about human rights and people on death row. At this point you may be wondering what this has to do with a 1960s Central League match, but it will all make sense - eventually. Put in 'Bahrain', 'Uzbekistan' and 'penalty' and you get a completely different picture: 'FIFA invalidates Uzbekistan-Bahrain result; match to be replayed.' Now that's more like it.

On 3rd September 2005, during the first leg of a World Cup Asian zone play-off match between the two countries, a controversial decision was taken by the referee, which is best summed up by the FIFA report:

1)	At the score of 1-0 in favour of Uzbekistan, in the 39th minute of the match, the referee decided to award a penalty kick to Uzbekistan;

2)	The penalty kick was taken and led to goal in favour of Uzbekistan;

3)	Before the penalty kick was carried out, an Uzbek player entered the penalty area;

4)	Consequently, the referee awarded an indirect free-kick to the Bahrain team;

5)	However, in such a situation, the Laws of the Game require the referee to order the penalty kick to be retaken.

The match finished 2-0 and the Uzbekistan FA appealed on the basis that the referee had erroneously applied the laws of the game, and the match should actually be awarded to them 3-0. FIFA disagreed and said the match should be replayed. That game finished 1-1 and the goalless draw in the second leg meant Bahrain progressed. Uzbekistan probably wished they had not appealed in the first place. FIFA stated that the referee's decision was 'unprecedented.' But FIFA – understandably perhaps - did not have an observer at St James'

Park for the visit of Everton reserves to Newcastle in 1969.

Spiteful was probably the best way of describing meetings between the two clubs in the late 1960s. The dismissals of central defender Ollie Burton and Gordon West at Newcastle in October 1967 are discussed elsewhere, and at Goodison in the same season Alan Ball was sent off in an equally bad-tempered game. Even the visit of Everton reserves to Newcastle in March 1966 was a riotous affair. Ninety seconds from time the Everton winger Aiden Maher was sent sprawling by John Craggs. The Blues trainer ran onto the pitch to speak to the referee, who immediately got together with his linesman and sent Craggs off. Whilst all this was going on, Newcastle's Albert Bennett and Everton's Gerry Glover were engaged in a wrestling match on the floor, and he dismissed both of them as well.

Three years later, for the final reserve fixture of the campaign there were some familiar names in the Everton second-string line-up, with all seeing first-team action during their Blues career: Barnett, Turner, Darcy, Brindle, Bennett, Whittle, Humphreys, Darracott, Lyons, Styles, Jones (G). The game was described in the *Daily Post* as one 'full of fouls, displays of bad temper and incredible decisions by the referee.'

The visitors began the game well and an Alan Whittle free-kick caused some trouble for the Newcastle keeper, who let the ball slip from his hands and was lucky to see Gerry Humphreys – the only survivor from the punch-up three years before - fire the loose ball just wide. The match swung from end-to-end until Everton stunned the hosts with three goals within the space of seven minutes. First of all Mick Lyons netted from a powerful header and then Billy Brindle shot from 30 yards, which the Newcastle keeper Clarke tried to push out but only succeeded in pushing over the line. On 41 minutes an Alan Whittle shot appeared to be covered by the Newcastle keeper until Cowan stuck out a foot and deflected the ball into his own net.

A minute before half-time came a quite incredible incident. The referee correctly awarded a penalty to the home side for a handball offence by an Everton player. Alan Duffy of Newcastle coolly slotted past Barnett but the referee disallowed the goal and pointed to the edge of the penalty area where his team-mate Keith Tyson was deemed to have been encroaching. The referee, Mr Rawdon, did not order a re-take but instead awarded a free-kick in Everton's favour at the point of encroachment, with complete disregard to the laws of the game.

The Newcastle players were outraged and were still arguing as they left the field for half-time shortly after. The referee went into both dressing rooms at half-time to apologise to both sets of players.

The bad feeling persisted both on and off the pitch after the break. There were continuous arguments between the Everton bench and spectators, and just before the hour the police were called to the ground. Arthur Proudler, the Everton trainer, was ordered to the tunnel where he was met by the local constabulary and eventually escorted away from St James' Park for his own safety. All this in a reserve match.

Newcastle pressed hard in the second half and were awarded with goals for Guthrie after 70 minutes and then ironically for Duffy, from the spot, a quarter of an hour from the end. But Everton held on for a memorable, and controversial, victory.

Police take a hand

The *Newcastle Evening Chronicle Pink* reported the following from the Newcastle United v Everton reserve fixture of May 1969: 'There was an amazing scene...where the Everton trainer was escorted up the tunnel by a police sergeant.

'He had been arguing with some Newcastle players from the touchline as well as shouting instructions to his own (team) when a police sergeant came up to him.

'A heated argument appeared to follow during which the trainer shouted for the referee. The referee came over and after a quick conference the Everton trainer was dragged, resisting all the while down the tunnel by the police sergeant.

'He then moved into the directors' box to watch the rest of the game and when spotted there by the crowd they shouted at him from the paddock.'

The best reserve game never played

Sixteen days before the debacle at Newcastle there had been an equally shambolic reserve match at Goodison – well nearly anyway. The match was scheduled for an afternoon kick-off on a Thursday afternoon. A larger than average crowd – it was the Easter holidays – were present, the home side were dressed and the match officials were also kitted out. Something was missing though – Leeds United reserves, the opponents. Why was that? Because they were still in Yorkshire. Frantic Everton officials phoned Elland Road and discovered that Leeds were under the impression that the match was an evening kick-off and so they could not turn up. Everyone had to leave the ground, and the match was postponed and rescheduled for eight days later – the teams drawing 1-1. But there was an even better story about the non-event that has recently surfaced.

In the week that the final manuscript to this book was due, this 'match' was casually mentioned to a friend of over 20 years, who revealed for the first time his own tale from that day: 'I went to that game with a lad from school. We were outside the Gwladys Street End when we were approached by an Everton official, who said they needed someone to sit in the Gwladys Street Stand – which was closed – and return the ball if it was kicked there. As it meant free entry we both agreed. We were sat down for 10 minutes but at 2.55 there was an announcement that the fixture had been postponed due to circumstances beyond the club's control. We stayed there for a bit, but when trying to leave we discovered that all the exits from the stand were boarded up. We were locked in Goodison Park! After an hour of banging on walls and doors – and some mischievous thoughts about hiding there for the next home match – we managed to climb onto the terrace, but by then everyone had left. After shouting for a while a member of staff came to our rescue. For our troubles the club kindly paid us two shillings and sixpence each in compensation. It was all a bit bizarre.'

A crowded Gwladys Street End circa 1960 - a completely different scene to that experienced by two youngsters at a reserve game

A six-second goal

Remarkable start
Everton 1-2 Manchester United
FA Youth Cup third round, 30th December, 1969

Goals in the opening seconds of a game have a sense of the surreal about them, neither players nor spectators being fully prepared for the impact of the ball finding the net at such an early stage of the game. The claims to scoring the fastest goal ever are many and varied, especially those from the days when timings were unofficial and television was absent. In this country it is generally accepted that the fastest goal scored in a first-team game is after six seconds, with three players holding a share of the record: Albert Mundy (Aldershot, 1958), Barrie Jones (Torquay, 1962) and Keith Smith (Crystal Palace, 1964). Jim Fryatt's famous, alleged, four-second goal for Bradford PA against Tranmere in 1965 has since been rejected, as contemporary press reports indicate it was significantly longer.

Goodison Park has seen more than its fair share of first-minute goals, including an 11-second goal by Colin Clarke for Bournemouth in September 1985, which is believed to be the fastest in a major domestic cup competition in this country. This was part of a nightmare sequence, when the Blues conceded goals in the opening seconds in five matches during the space of two months. Things had got out of hand so much that, before a home match against Chelsea, Howard Kendall announced: "Whatever you do today, don't concede in the first minute." The score after 53 seconds... Everton 0-1 Chelsea.

However, few have left a greater impression than the one scored by David Johnson against Manchester United in an FA Youth Cup tie at Goodison on the penultimate evening of the 1960s. The Mancunian youngsters had journeyed to Everton for the second consecutive season, having won 3-1 in a quarter-final replay earlier in the year. Their line-up featured future England international Brian Greenhoff, whilst the Blues had future first-teamers Ronnie Goodlass, Mick Lyons and, of course, Johnson himself.

The start of the game was amazing and it left 'United, and most of the 4,451 spectators, staggered,' according to the *Daily Post*. Lyons and Alan Wilson took the kick-off, passing to left-half Bryn Jones, whose first touch sent the ball directly up the centre of the pitch where, from a position just outside of the box, Johnson fired a fierce shot past United keeper Billy Carrick. After just three touches and SIX seconds the ball had found its way into the United net. Anyone reaching their seat after 10 seconds would have missed the goal.

It was understandable that, after a barely believable and historic start, the rest of the game sunk into an anti-climax. A strong United team – with Greenhoff outstanding – got themselves back into the game with a goal by Eric Young just after half-time, and scored the winner after 67 minutes through centre-forward Jim Hall following confusion in the Everton defence. Although the Blues battled hard with Lyons – then a rampaging centre-forward – causing difficulty for the opposition, the United defence held firm and deservedly entered the next round.

Johnson went on to a long and distinguished career, becoming the first player to score for both teams in a Merseyside derby. He set two other similar Everton records in the first team – the fastest booking (10 seconds after coming on as a substitute at Maine Road in March 1971) and the fastest goal by a substitute (20 seconds after entering the fray against Watford in January 1983). Neither compared to this astonishing feat – the quickest goal in a match at Goodison Park.

POSTSCRIPT:

The next Everton home programme pointed to research that had shown that, unless the ball is kicked directly in from the kick-off, the fastest time a goal could be scored in is about six seconds. Johnson's goal was officially credited at that time by the club, although the *Daily Post* gave the time at one second less. Sir Matt Busby was present and he said that it was 'one of the quickest I have seen.'

The *Manchester Evening News* report interestingly gave the time at 25 seconds, which confirms what has long been suspected – watches run at a different pace at that end of the M62, especially the referee's during injury-time at Old Trafford when United are trailing.

Fastest goals at Goodison

6 seconds

David Johnson

Everton v Manchester United (FA Youth Cup, 30th December 1969)

   March 2008 saw Ayegbeni Yakubu add his own footnote in the fastest goals at Goodison list. His opening goal against Portsmouth in a 3-1 Premier League win, although timed at 47 seconds, was actually scored in just eight seconds of open play following a stoppage after Everton had been awarded a free-kick.

11 seconds

Colin Clarke

Everton v **Bournemouth** (League Cup, 25th September 1985)

   The ball is played from the kick-off to former Liverpool reserve Colin Russell, who nutmegs Kevin Ratcliffe by the by-line, before pulling the ball back for Colin Clarke to volley in from an acute angle. The goal came just four days after Kenny Dalglish had netted after just 20 seconds of the derby match on the ground.

13 seconds

Chris Sutton

Everton v **Blackburn Rovers** (Premier League, 1st April 1995)

   Following an exchange of headers with Alan Shearer, Sutton breaks free and scores the then fastest goal in Premiership history.

14 seconds

Howard Kendall

Everton v Chelsea (First Division, 28th March 1970)

   Three months after Johnson's goal, the future Blues boss scores the fastest goal by an Everton player on the ground in a first-team match. The ball is played into the Chelsea box by Sandy Brown from the kick-off and, after being headed out by John Dempsey, the ball runs to Howard who slots home after beating two men. Everton win 5-2 and clinch the title four days later.

15 seconds

Jackie Balmer

Everton v **Liverpool** (First Division, 16th February 1938)

Unofficially timings for this goal vary from five seconds to a more likely 15 seconds, given the passage of play from the kick-off. The ball is touched by three Liverpool players before being moved to Shafto on the right and from his cross, Balmer nips in to fire home. The Blues eventually lose 3-1.

15 seconds

David Cross

Everton v **Norwich City** (League Cup, 30th October 1973)

Three weeks before their own-goal fest at Carrow Road, the home team crash out of the League Cup at Goodison. Briggs and Colin Suggett combine to leave the bearded striker with an easy opportunity to fire past a stranded (wasn't he always stranded?) David Lawson.

15 seconds

Bleasdale

Everton reserves v **Sheffield Wednesday reserves** (Central League, 16th April 1977)

The unknown reserve scored for the visitors from the kick-off

19 seconds

Bill Nicholson

England v Portugal (Friendly, 19th May 1951)

A crowd of 53,000 were present when good work from Henry Cockburn, Metcalf and Stan Pearson enable Bill Nicholson to score from 18 yards with his first touch in international football

Dave's debuts

David Johnson's other claim to fame was his penchant for scoring on his debut for Everton at all levels. Although often mentioned in books, the definitive list of matches has never been published, but for the first time here it is (opposite page):

FA Youth Cup	Tranmere Rovers (a)	27th November 1967
Central League	Blackburn Rovers (h)	9th August 1969
League	Burnley (a)	9th January 1971
FA Cup	Derby County (h)	13th February 1971
European Cup	Panathanaikos (h)	9th March 1971
League Cup	Southampton (a)	7th September 1971
The derby	Liverpool (h)	13th November 1971

Whilst at Ipswich, Johnson also scored on his England debut against Wales at Wembley in May 1975

And what is the former Everton striker doing with Ronnie Biggs?

In 1989 Johnson was one of a number of former professionals who travelled to Sao Paulo for a multinational 'seniors' tournament. On a trip to Sugerloaf Mountain the party – also including Duncan McKenzie and Alan Whittle – bumped into Ronnie Biggs, who was selling souvenirs. Johnson and the 'Great Train robber' had their photo taken together and it was published, rather incongruously, in an Everton home programme in February 1989.

Howard Kendall (left) and David Johnson (right), pictured with Ronnie Biggs - The Everton duo were quick off the mark for the Blues

7 9 7 9 8 9 9 7

'An avalanche in the snow'
Everton 8-0 Southampton
First Division, 20th November, 1971

Reasons for the demise of the 1970 Championship team have been subject to much conjecture over the years, from career-ending injuries (Brian Labone) to the impact of the 1970 World Cup. What cannot be disputed is that the side did have one last hurrah, one last glimpse of the magic, skill and power that had brought the title, won, in Harry Catterick's words "by playing pure football, there were no destroyers in the team."

That game came 19 months after a 2-0 win over West Brom had brought a seventh league title and promise that the team could set the standards for English football in the following decade. Southampton were the visitors on a first snow-filled day of the winter and realistically there was little to be gleaned from the form of either side to suggest that anything out-of-the-ordinary was on the horizon. There was a certain symmetry to the Blues' position at the start of the day, lying 17th in the table after 17 games with just 13 points and 13 goals (although the previous week had seen a hard-fought 1-0 derby win on the ground). The Saints were not exactly setting the world on fire, being one place ahead with 15 points.

The Everton team featured eight players who had won championship medals in 1970 as well as John McLaughlin, Peter Scott and the exciting local youngster David Johnson. For their part Southampton featured former Goodison favourite Jimmy Gabriel and a strong forward line of big Ron Davies, Mick Channon and 1976 FA Cup final hero Bobby Stokes.

The match started in a heavy snowstorm, and almost immediately Everton nearly grabbed the lead when Whittle prodded the ball past keeper Eric Martin only to see John McGrath kick off the line. It was very much an indication of things to come. There was no let-up in the pressure applied to the Saints goal from this point, with Ball particularly in fine fettle, and it was nearly 10 minutes until Gordon West touched the ball. Unsurprisingly after 13 minutes the home side went ahead, a long ball from Tommy Wright deceived Joe

Kirkup as it skidded off the wet turf and David Johnson was able to nip in and beat Martin at the near post.

It was 2-0 shortly after when fine combination play with Whittle gave Joe Royle a clean run on Martin and the big striker drilled a well-placed shot past the keeper. Martin was in action a minute later, this time saving well from a fierce shot by Ball. The one-way traffic continued at this point – Johnson, who was having the best game of his fledgling career, flashed a shot just wide and set up chances for both Whittle and Ball, which neither accepted. Shortly before the half-hour it was three, when a ball played deep from Kendall reached Whittle and the blonde-haired striker's through pass to Johnson was clinically finished off by the youngster from 12 yards out.

Five minutes before the break Royle scored Everton's fourth, and his second, when another cross from Kendall zipped across the wet pitch and wrong-footed the Southampton defence, leaving the England striker with a chance to flick the ball in from close range. Amazingly this was not the end to the first-half goal blitz – a minute before half-time the opposition defence was left short as they moved up en bloc for a free-kick, and when it was cleared it was Alan Ball who raced fully 60 yards unchallenged to slide the ball past Martin from the edge of the box. The Blues left the pitch to a standing ovation from the 29,000 crowd who, in a season characterised by its mediocrity, had witnessed a veritable feast.

Straight from the second-half kick-off Everton should have gone six-up when Ball shot narrowly wide from a neat back header by Royle and then Wright's shot following a corner hit the outside of the post. The one-way traffic was continuing with Southampton unable to retain possession for any length of time to trouble the Everton rearguard, and there was no surprise that on the hour Royle completed his hat-trick with a stunning half-volley from the edge of the box. If one man stood out in the massacre it was Ball, whose creative brilliance in the treacherous conditions was a highlight of the penultimate home appearance of the midfielder's Everton career.

Everton were now running riot and according to the *Daily Telegraph*, they: '...hardly put a foot wrong. Almost everything they attempted came off.' The paper also added that the home team's form meant that 'though a blizzard raged throughout the match, none of the crowd seemed to complain about the cold.'

Royle was to add a fourth on 72 minutes, which required the only bit of luck required by the home team in the afternoon. A shot from Ball was pushed out by Martin to Kendall, whose mis-hit fell invitingly into the path of the big striker and Royle nodded the ball home. (In 1977 Joe would also score four goals for Bristol City, and prior to Graeme Sharp he was the last player to achieve this particular feat for two different clubs in the top flight.) Alan Whittle was also enjoying an excellent game and it was clear, with the pressure off, that his team-mates were doing everything to get the blonde striker on the scoresheet.

They were to be disappointed as the rout was complete with five minutes left when Johnson capitalised on a misunderstanding between John McGrath and Eric Martin to score the eighth with a delightful chip over the hapless keeper. It was the youngster's first senior hat-trick and it remains the only post-War league match in which two Everton players had scored three or more goals each. It was also Southampton's biggest defeat for 44 years. For a second time in the afternoon, the Blues left the pitch to a thoroughly-deserved standing ovation, which was reflected on the famous photograph of the Goodison scoreboard at the end, which immortalised the shirt numbers of the scorers –

'7 9 7 9 8 9 9 7'

POSTSCRIPT:

This was undoubtedly one of the most freakish results in the club's history. To put it into the context of the time, it was the only league match out of 55 played between April 1971 and September 1972 that Everton scored more than two goals. The game accounted for over 20% of the total league tally for 1971-72, which is unprecedented for a top-flight club. The eight goals were scored in 72 minutes and the Blues' next eight league goals that season took 21 hours to score over 14 games until mid-March 1972.

Big Joe was a relieved man after the game: "All season Harry Catterick has been urging me to put more fire into my game. Even after I had scored my fourth goal, he was leaping up and down in the trainer's box, shouting at me to get more."

There is one other interesting story to relay about 20th November 1971 – a player in another fixture scored more goals personally than Everton. This was the day when former Liverpool reserve Ted MacDougall famously scored nine goals for Bournemouth in their 11-2 win over Margate in the FA Cup. Coincidentally that night's *Liverpool Echo* printed a letter from a Liverpool fan who was frustrated that MacDougall had been allowed to leave the club.

However, no book about strange events would be complete without a mention of the poor Margate keeper in that match, the peerless Chic Brodie - a man who could offer careers advice on what to do when faced with the unusual on the pitch, and whose own exploits put him on a different level to any player featured here. Brodie, who sadly died in 2000, survived when a hand-grenade was tossed into the penalty area at Millwall in 1965, and was present when the complete goal frame collapsed in a match at Lincoln – which was a problem, as he was standing directly underneath it at the time. The cursed keeper's league career was ended after injuring a knee following a collision with a sheepdog, which had strayed onto the playing area, when he was playing for Brentford in 1970. His comments after the match were priceless: "The dog may have only been a small one, but it was a solid one."

The scoreboard spells out the score (above) while Alan Ball (below) punishes the Saints at Goodison Park

A brawl at the Palace

'The nearest I've seen to a riot'
Crystal Palace 2-2 Everton
FA Cup third round, 15th January, 1972

There has always been a bit of bad blood between Everton and Palace, culminating in a couple of spiteful matches in the early 1990s. The origins of this rivalry stems back to a bitterly-contested FA Cup match at Selhurst Park in 1972, when the referee appealed to the crowd to curb their hostility or he would have no option but to abandon the contest. The *Daily Telegraph* would later say: '...this was the game that died of shame – the shame of undisciplined players and a referee who failed to impose his outburst on untamed violence', with the *Sunday Times* being equally critical: 'This was a shameful match, continual fouling accompanied by a hateful sound of malice and rage from 30,000-odd spectators.'

The 1971-72 season had seen a typical period of introspection for the English game, as several years' unruly behaviour on the pitch and, after being on the periphery of the game in the 1960s, the rise of hooliganism off it, had forced the authorities to take action. The first response was for the Football League in the summer of 1971 to adopt the continental approach to enforcing the laws of the game – in other words, act by the letter of the law. Players would now be cautioned for technical offences, tactical fouls and deliberate handling.

By the time the Blues visited Selhurst Park in the New Year, this deterrent had clearly not worked. The booking count had increased dramatically – up to 1,100 by that stage of the season, with mass appeals from players causing a bureaucratic headache – and had the then PFA chairman, Derek Dougan, calling for action: "The livelihoods of our members has been put in jeopardy; we are getting away from common sense and instead finding chaos and confusion."

The Everton side that afternoon was a pale shadow of the team that had romped to the title just 18 months before. Although Harvey and Kendall remained, Alan Ball had moved to Arsenal the month before and the line-up included inexperienced players such as Peter Scott, Terry Darracott, David Johnson and a young Mick Lyons. To make matters worse, trainer-coach Tommy Casey took charge as Harry Catterick convalesced following his recent heart-attack.

Palace were similarly struggling, which probably didn't help, although they did feature former Liverpool full-back Peter Wall, the aptly named Gerry Queen – 'Queen involved in punch-up at the Palace' – and two former Celtic players; Willie Wallace, of the 1967 'Lisbon Lions', and big John Hughes, brother of Sunderland's 1973 FA Cup-winner, Billy. Both were to play a leading role in the anarchy that followed (Hughes was essentially made persona non grata by Jock Stein at Celtic Park after missing a sitter in the 1970 European Cup final against Feyenoord, which the Glasgow side lost 2-1).

It was Joe Royle, of all people, who started it all. A thumping challenge in the early moments on John Jackson left the Palace keeper limping for the rest of the game, and also left him with a lump of congealed blood 'the size of a man's fist' at the top of his thigh. Colin Harvey then felt the heat, requiring several minutes' treatment for a low blow to the stomach following a strong challenge from McCormick. After coming back onto the pitch, he immediately suffered another foul from Kellard, with the Palace defender being booked, as was Joe Royle for foul language to the referee, Mr Tommy Dawes. Then Hughes was booked for a heavy foul on Royle, having already been spoken to by the ref.

During this phase of the game full-back John McLaughlin was left comatose on the pitch following a right hook from a Palace player. Such was the untold level of aggression that fouls were now happening every 60 seconds. But it was not all one way, Palace midfielder Mel Blyth required treatment off the pitch with blood seeping from a head wound.

In the chaos there was actually some football being played, with a young Everton side dominating for long periods. Just before half-time though, in the several minutes added on for injuries, Palace broke clear and Wallace fired home. Five minutes into the second half the Blues deservedly levelled, with a fine run and a cross from the left by McLaughlin being finished off determinedly by Alan Whittle, after the blonde striker's initial effort had bounced off the bar and rolled across the line. It was McLaughlin who was actually singled out for praise by the *Sunday Times* 'as one of the few players whose football was of a high standard.' Although that statement may surprise a few who are long in the tooth, the next bit from the same paper surely carries some resonance with those who followed the Blues at that time: 'McLaughlin is only 23, but because of his bald head he looks like a man who is past it.'

If anything, the intensity of the battle had increased, with a particular period of fierce tackles resulting in John Hughes, who could be awkward and clumsy at the best of times, being dismissed on 53 minutes for a horrible challenge on David Johnson, one that sent the young Blues striker flying five yards and reeling in agony. This was the former Celtic man's second dismissal: his first had been in an even more feisty encounter - the 1967 World Club Championship match against Racing Club of Argentina.

After 65 minutes, Gerry Queen – on his birthday – was the next name in the referee's book, for a dreadful foul on Lyons. Three spectators then invaded the pitch with the specific intention of attacking Mr Dawes, who immediately left the playing area having been protected by the combined efforts of the police, players and stewards. Several moments later an announcement over the PA system warned spectators that any further incursions would lead to the game being abandoned – although such was their mood, the noise drowned out the message. Whilst all this was going on, police snatch squads entered the crowd to arrest fans fighting amongst themselves.

The game now entered a relatively tranquil period, with both sides coming close on several occasions until Wallace scored his second, with a quarter of an hour remaining, after a fine through ball by Bobby Kellard. But once again the Blues replied immediately, with Harvey, who had enjoyed an excellent match, driving home through a crowd of players from the edge of the box. The game fizzled out to a draw, although there was still time for Whittle to be booked for a foul on the long-suffering Jackson. 'It was all deplorable and best forgotten,' was one paper's verdict.

The following few days were full of recriminations from both clubs, with blame being apportioned to all sides. Mr A.J. Wait, the Palace chairman, was first out of the blocks, blaming the referee and the opposition: "…I thought he booked everything including the corner flag…there was no football and Everton were the culprits." He also added with a touch of humour that "we shall have to get the armour out and polish it up for the replay." John Moores took a darker view: "We used to talk about the South Americans, but now we are getting just as bad." But the final words go to Bert Head, the Palace boss: "It was a frightening sight – the nearest I've ever seen to a riot on a British football ground in all my career."

POSTSCRIPT:

After attempts from both clubs to control the subsequent ill-feeling, the replay at Goodison passed off without major incident, with Everton winning an entertaining match 3-2 - 'No bookings, no nasty fouls, only thrills,' according to the *Daily Mirror* - thanks to a 37-second goal by Peter Scott, the fastest for the Toffees in the competition in the post-War era. There was a new referee, Mr Paul Smith, who handled the game impeccably and, in what was perhaps a football first, there was a loudspeaker announcement at the end of the game, praising the referee 'for handling a potentially explosive replay.'

Spurs ended Everton's run with a 2-0 victory at Goodison in the fifth round. That season couldn't end soon enough for the club, with only two league wins being collected in 17 matches after Everton had survived the 'Selhurst savagery.'

Crystal Palace goalkeeper John Jackson (above, top right) and Everton's Colin Harvey (above right) feel the pain at Selhurst Park. Above left: The 23-year-old John 'Tiger' McLaughlin, described by the Sunday Times as a man who 'because of his bald head, he looks like a man who is past it'

Four disowned goals

'An afternoon of multiple own goals'
Norwich City 1-3 Everton
First Division, 17th November, 1973

In these days of various camera angles and what is known as the 'Dubious Goals Panel' in the Premiership, it is usually pretty easy to come to a final decision over determining who can be correctly credited with a goal. In the past this was not so straightforward, of course. Prior to the modern era the tendency was to award goals to the attacker rather than the defender – this explains why Sandy Brown's own goal at Goodison in 1969 is generally acknowledged as the first in derby matches, even though an examination of previous match reports against the old enemy shows that, using today's rules, several goals would have been classed as self-inflicted (an example being Everton full-back William Balmer's header into his own net against Liverpool at Goodison in a 1902 FA Cup tie).

The lack of evidence has also caused a nightmare to statisticians, with the same goal sometimes being credited to different players in the press, club records (which understandably seem to favour the attacker) and other authoritative reference guides. Such confusion has led to several anomalies.

Which leads us nicely into the Norwich v Everton clash at Carrow Road in 1973. This was the home team's second season in the top flight, with their first-ever game being a 1-1 draw against the Blues in August 1972. The Toffees had started the 1973-74 campaign (the first under Billy Bingham) with a flourish and stood fifth at the start of play. The man in the Canaries hot-seat was the Birkenhead-born, poker-faced former Everton player Ron Saunders, of whom it was once rather unfairly said that the possession of a sense of humour was an optional extra. Saunders had started life as an apprentice at Goodison in the late 1940s, and once scored eight goals in a 'B' team match against Earle. After leaving he played for several clubs, and was involved in a memorable incident at Goodison when with Portsmouth, which was described earlier.

The away team started the game confidently enough with Mick Buckley, who was enjoying the best spell of his Everton career, dominating the midfield, but up front Joe Harper, who was having a lean time in front of goal, failed to take advantage of several opportunities. As the half wore on the game became a real war of attrition for both sides, leaving the East Anglian crowd praying for action and entertainment. 'There is a numbing mediocrity about Norwich that is not easy to define,' was the view of one observer. A moribund half led to both teams being booed as they left the field.

Five minutes into the second half and the home side had something to cheer at last, Norwich moving menacingly down the Blues' right flank with the resulting cross being headed firmly past David Lawson not by a Canaries attacker, but by the Blues full-back, John 'Tiger' McLaughlin. It was the Scot's second own goal of his Everton career, the first being in the fraught 4-0 defeat at Anfield 18 months earlier (this match also featured a 32-second own goal by Tommy Wright, with the Blues full-back netting a further effort after 35 seconds of the match against Manchester City seven days later). McLaughlin's blooper was described as the 'most studied, perfectly executed own goal of the year' in the *Daily Mail* whilst the *Sunday Times* – never a paper to pass up an opportunity to comment on the Scot – was equally enthusiastic: 'It would have beaten any goalkeeper in the world. An own goal for the connoisseur.' Their journalist also commented that 'McLaughlin played like a man having a nervous breakdown after the goal, spoiling one of the most cultivated left-back displays I have seen for a long time.'

Everton got back into the match within an instant. A fine move through the middle saw Dave Clements let fly from 25 yards and his shot took a wicked deflection off the heel of Duncan Forbes and span past the despairing dive of goalkeeper Kevin Keelan. On 69 minutes a similar move, with this time Mike Bernard firing home from the same position, saw the ball taking a big deflection off Dave Stringer.

The Blues were now in the box seat and their continuing pressure paid off when they completed a 3-1 win, two minutes from time, when Buckley's cross was headed home, in McLaughlin-esque style, by Duncan Forbes for his second own goal of the afternoon. The Blues maintained control of the game and they left East Anglia with both points after a slightly unusual encounter to say the least.

POSTSCRIPT:

After the match, the first talking point concerned who should be credited with the afternoon's goals? It was agreed by everyone that both McLaughlin's and Forbes' headed efforts were clearly own goals. It was also recommended by the referee (Mr Bosi, of Codsall) that Forbes should also be credited with Everton's first when he deflected Clements' shot – thus doubling Forbes' goal tally for the afternoon. This was the generally held view of the press. 'Two obvious own goals by Forbes,' was the *Daily Mail's* line.

However, Norwich officials were adamant Mike Bernard's shot should also be classed as an own goal. Captain Dave Stringer told the press that "all three of the Everton goals were deflections." Stringer's motives were unclear at the time, although he was probably trying to confirm the view that the Toffees were lucky to take the points. "It was my goal and no-one is going to take it away from me," said Bernard, who was having none of it. Ron Saunders was wryly humorous: "I don't know if four own goals qualifies for the *Guinness Book of Records*, but it was certainly an unusual way to lose."

Whatever the view, this game remains the only Everton match to feature own goals from both sides. But the real drama of the afternoon was still to come. There was an incredible story of the post-match events that concerned the sacking of the Norwich manager – in full view of shocked diners. A door connecting a dining room to the club boardroom was open when Saunders went to see his club chairman after the game. In front of startled guests the following confrontation took place:

Arthur South (chairman): Manager, when you come into the boardroom you address yourself or say good afternoon to the directors.
Saunders: (Inaudible reply).
AS: Well if that's the way you feel then the sooner you get out the better. Well you might as well hand in your resignation now.
Saunders: (Inaudible reply).
AS: I'm used to dealing with children like you. I can handle children like you.

South then left the room and, in full view of bemused onlookers, Saunders wrote his resignation in the boardroom. It was an eccentric end to the day. Saunders then moved to Manchester City and Aston Villa where, in the 1977 League Cup final, he was to have the last laugh – if that were possible for him – on the Blue half of Merseyside. He lifted the title with Villa in 1981 when he was also Harry Catterick's choice to replace Gordon Lee. 'The Cat' described Saunders as like a man in his own image: "I have a high regard for him. I like his style, the way he works, the teams he produces. He's a bit of a loner, he's forthright and he wants to be in charge."

Roxburgh's afternoon to forget

Setting aside Duncan Forbes, only one player has been universally attributed with two own goals in a single Everton match, and that was the Blackburn left-back Bob Roxburgh, in a league game at Goodison on 23rd February 1929. After 15 minutes the defender and Everton's Tommy White both went for the same ball, and Roxburgh's back pass to Crawford in the visitor's goal was misplaced under pressure and evaded the stranded keeper. Ten minutes from time a powerful shot from Alec Troup was directed into the roof of the net at the near post by the full-back to complete an unwanted double.

Andy O'Brien's own goal in Everton's 1-0 victory at Portsmouth in January 2006 was also the second of his career against the Blues, after netting one for Bradford in the FA Cup at Goodison in January 1997. The Republic of Ireland international is the only player to have conceded own goals for two different clubs against Everton.

A third of an own goal each...

...could have been the conclusion reached after Everton's visit to Old Trafford in April 1976. Alex Forsyth's free-kick hit Ken McNaught's head before striking Mick Lyons in the face and then rebounded off the back of Roger Kenyon before crossing the line.

Billy Balmer: Own goal king

William Balmer was a classy, but robust right-back who played for, and captained, the club at the turn of the 20th century. An England international, he made 331 appearances for Everton and was part of the 1906 FA Cup-winning side. Balmer also had a propensity for scoring own goals, at a time when only 20-yard screamers into your own net were counted. In the 20 years following the introduction of league football in 1888, Everton players were credited with conceding just 19 own goals, and Balmer alone accounted for eight of them. He clearly leads the all-time table of Everton players with the most own goals:

William Balmer	8
Tommy Wright	5
Dave Watson	4
T.G. Jones	4

Double trouble

Two Everton players have scored own goals in the same game on three separate occasions. At Tottenham in 1960 both Johnny King and Brian Harris found the wrong net, and Tommy Wright and John McLaughlin did the same in March 1972 at Anfield in a 4-0 loss. The most recent occurrence was at Craven Cottage in May 2003, when the Toffees' European hopes were damaged by a 2-0 loss with Alan Stubbs and Richard Wright being culpable.

How an own goal was not credited...

...during the course of Everton's visit to Newcastle in March 1971 baffled all those present. Dai Davies was making his debut and, after 13 minutes, the home team's Wyn Davies powerfully met a corner from 'Jinky' Smith. With the Welshman beaten, Colin Harvey was on hand to head off the line but the ball struck the Everton keeper, who was standing with his back to goal, on the arm and rebounded in. After the match the referee incredibly awarded the goal to Bobby Moncur, who appeared to be standing in the goalmouth minding his own business according to incredulous observers. At least Davies was spared the embarrassment of being credited with an own goal within a quarter of an hour of his debut.

Rowdy Yates in booking bonanza

New Brittish record at Goodison
Everton 1-1 Chelsea
First Division, 18th October, 1974

Everyone remembers the 1974-75 season. That was the campaign when Billy Bingham's expensively assembled, but pretty ordinary ensemble – compared to, say, Gordon Lee's side of three years later – scaled the heights of the First Division, only to fall off their perch thanks to three defeats by the relegated Carlisle United and Luton Town.

But there is an interesting statistic about that campaign that is relevant to this particular match, in that only 11 players were booked against Everton in the league - those were the days when, even allowing for stricter guidelines, players were given carte blanche to foul indiscriminately and the ref would produce his notebook only in instances of GBH. When stating 11 players were booked, that does not allow for the Chelsea game at Goodison - the reason why this is the case will soon become apparent.

The Toffees went into the game having enjoyed a solid, if slightly tedious start to the campaign, with just one game lost in the opening 13 matches, but eight had been drawn. Chelsea were in a state of crisis, the Kings Road glory team of the early 1970s had broken up and the failure to find adequate replacements had seen Dave Sexton sent to the managerial guillotine a fortnight before (coincidentally Sexton was enjoying his first game as boss of QPR on this day, against Liverpool).

The main talk on the Blue half of Merseyside was the banishment of Joe Royle to the reserves at Burnley, a sign many surmised that would lead to a move away from Goodison (Mick Lyons would take his place). Ron Suart was the Chelsea caretaker-manager, a man who whilst manager of Blackpool had sanctioned the transfer of Alan Ball to Goodison. The referee was Mr John Yates of Redditch, who had a day he would never forget.

Chelsea began the game in spirited fashion, and it was no surprise that they were 1-0 ahead after six minutes, when a John Hollins cross was headed into the goalmouth by Chris Garland, and after Dai Davies fumbled the ball, Charlie Cooke nipped in to score. The home team immediately went on the offensive with Pearson and Connolly both heading over from good positions. By half-time it looked like it was going to be one of those days, as Martin Dobson and Connolly again both fired wide from seven yards out.

The action really started after 56 minutes. A Chelsea player went down injured and trainer Norman Medhurst ran onto the pitch to provide treatment. However, a recent instruction meant that trainers entering the pitch to treat players, without permission, could be booked, which is exactly what happened. This was despite Horace Yates in the *Daily Post* claiming that 'he had been given a clear indication by the referee to attend to the player.'

Four minutes later things took a really dramatic turn – for the early 1970s – when four Chelsea players entered the book for failing to retreat 10 yards at an Everton free-kick. Then in the 71st minute Gary Jones came on as a substitute for Jim Pearson, and immediately crossed for Lyons, whose header hit the side netting. Shortly afterwards Garland became the fifth Chelsea player booked for persistent fouling. Then big Mickey Droy – reckoned to be the heaviest player of the time and, when bearded, one who looked suspiciously like the wrestler Giant Haystacks – cleared off the line from Connolly, before Tommy Baldwin at the other end had a goal disallowed for offside.

Six minutes from time, just when it looked as though Chelsea were home and dry, Gary Jones crossed from the left and although Lyons was floored initially, Mr Yates decreed that it was the foul by Droy on Hurst that warranted a penalty. Mike Bernard was the usual taker but he handed over the duty to Gary Jones: "You can take it if you want," Jones would admit afterwards, and thankfully the substitute coolly slotted home. It was his first goal after four years and 28 appearances for the Blues.

Shortly after Droy became the sixth Chelsea player to enter Mr Yates' rapidly filled-up notebook, two minutes from time for a foul on Mick Buckley. It was not an especially dirty game, and even Droy was 'less intimidating than usual' according to *The Daily Telegraph*. Two minutes later and the game was all over at 1-1. But it wasn't – on the way off the pitch John Dempsey was booked, or appeared to be booked, as the players left the playing area, although it would turn out he had been 'sent off.'

POSTSCRIPT:

Few, if any Everton matches have seen so much coverage in the national press as this one. The *Daily Mail* saw fit to fill the entire back page of Monday's edition to coverage of the game and its aftermath (as well as giving Yates 1/10 for his performance). Eight bookings for one side in a league match, including the trainer, was unheard of. Not only that but Dempsey's was actually classed as a sending-off offence, making him the only player dismissed in an Everton match after the final whistle. It was also pointed out that the home side did not have a single player booked.

As you can imagine, the referee was the centre of attention. Mr Yates was tight-lipped though, his after-match comments covered the penalty solely: "A player was tripped in the box," was all he would say. On the Monday though he was more verbose: "It was played in good spirit, but I'm just carrying out my directive as instructed by the league." As for Dempsey's dismissal, he was bullish: "He was reported for what he said as the teams were leaving the field", Mr Yates explained, "and although he was not technically sent off, it will be reported as a sending-off offence as if it had happened during the game." Dempsey was subsequently charged with bringing the game into disrepute (on the same day as QPR's Terry Mancini, who had famously took his shorts off in front of the directors' box after a win against Ipswich).

Dempsey was not a happy bunny: "As we came off, all's I said to the referee was that a player could have a broken leg and he wouldn't let the trainer on." Trainer Norman Medhurst also complained that Mr Yates "...let play continue when one of the Everton players punched Ian Britton in the face and got away with it." The Chelsea chairman, Brian Mears was flummoxed and said there would be an internal inquiry into Mr Yates' performance, although nothing would eventually come of it.

There was no murmur from the Everton side; mind you there was no need to. One player did jokingly comment after the game that the only person not booked was the St John Ambulance-man.

As for Mr Yates, well he became a bit of a celebrity in his own right, and he was photographed in the *Daily Mirror* displaying his historic notebook from the game. The Football League were not amused and suspended him for three matches, although they stressed this was because he should not have allowed his notes to be published, and not due to his performance at Goodison.

The eight players booked for one team were a record for any game in Britain at the time, and Chelsea have continued to have disciplinary problems since then against the Toffees - the London club have had 10 players dismissed, which is a record against Everton (accurate at December, 2006).

Chelsea plan
mass appeal

The above headline, taken from the *Liverpool Daily Post* the following Monday, was an indication of the London club's feeling of injustice over their record number of bookings. As their caretaker manager Ron Suart reflected: "It seems strange that so many of our players were booked." Incidentally John Dempsey, who was sent off after the match had ended, admitted that he called the referee "an idiot."

Norman Medhurst wasn't the first trainer booked at Goodison...an earlier example can be seen below.

Frank King, a former Everton trainer and keeper gets into trouble with referee L. Callaghan for running onto the field with his sponge to cool down his Luton players, August 1959. In the background Brian Harris receives treatment from Gordon Watson

Lights out at Goodison
'Match suspended as floodlights fail'
Everton 1-1 Manchester United
First Division, 22nd December, 1975

Floodlit football goes back longer than you would think – all the way back to the 19th century in fact. An Everton XI played a game against Manchester District on 27th November 1893 under 16 Wells lights, 15 years after Sheffield United used them for the first time. It was not until the 1950s however that floodlights became the norm for the game in this country; the Blues' first official match under them was at Newcastle in November 1956, whilst the first game at Goodison was famously to mark the 75th anniversary of the Liverpool County FA against our rivals from across the Park in 1957.

Rather surprisingly since then only three Everton matches have been hit by floodlight failure – and thankfully none were due to accusations concerning gambling syndicates. At White Hart Lane in December 1969 the match was abandoned due to the lights failing after 30 minutes. Since then two further games have been interrupted in this manner - but were still finished. The first was the clash against Manchester United at Goodison in 1975, three days before Christmas. After the Blues had begun the season well, they were languishing in mid-table for the visit of Tommy Docherty's exciting and dynamic young team. It was also significant for the long-overdue debut of Ronnie Goodlass, who had literally been waiting in the wings for several seasons as a replacement for Gary Jones, rumoured to be a scouting target for the watching England manager, Don Revie.

United swarmed all over the home side in the opening 10 minutes and could have scored on three occasions but for fine work by Dai Davies in the Everton goal. But just before the half-hour mark they went ahead with a beautifully-taken goal by Macari, a player who often saved his best performances for the Blue half of Merseyside. With his back to goal, the former Celtic player swivelled and hooked the ball beyond Davies into the top corner. The Toffees restored the equilibrium just before half-time when

Latchford turned home Bernard's free-kick after brave work from Hamilton - who was knocked-out unconscious after being kicked in the head - and Dobson. It was the sixth consecutive match in which 'the Latch' had found the net.

The incident that made this game unique in Goodison history occurred after 65 minutes when, during a scramble in the United box, the floodlights went out and plunged the ground into total darkness. The referee let play continue for several moments until calling a halt and immediately led the players from the ground. Radio Merseyside presenter Billy Butler was the tannoy announcer in those days at Goodison and his instructions were clear: "The club and police were scared of crowd unrest, so I was told to keep talking and entertain the crowd, so I told a few jokes. It must have worked because a few days later I got a letter of thanks from the Everton directors." After a gap of 14 minutes the players returned. The game continued to ebb and flow for the remaining 25 minutes with both defences on top while the sides showed no inclination to push forward in numbers which may have risked losing their hard-earned point.

POSTSCRIPT:

Two years later Gordon Lee's outfit were hanging onto the coat-tails of Brian Clough's Nottingham Forest during the course of a 22-match unbeaten run which would last from August until a 6-2 defeat at Goodison on Boxing Day to Manchester United.

Appropriately it was Bonfire Night 1977 when the Blues travelled to the Baseball Ground to visit a Derby County side falling alarmingly from their two Championship triumphs of the first half of the decade. Tommy Docherty was in the hot seat and, although the Rams were clearly ailing, he could still call on veterans such as the prolific Kevin Hector and stylish full-back David Nish - the man who in 1972 took over Alan Ball's mantle of the most expensive domestic player - as well as Bruce Rioch, who had recently returned to the club from his brief but eventful spell at Goodison. Rioch had left the previous week, having played his last game for Everton just seven days before. The Blues featured Trevor Ross, who was essentially a replacement for Rioch, in an unfamiliar right-back role on his debut.

The country at the time was in the midst of a month-long power dispute - a regular feature of 1970s Britain - that limited the electricity supply. Sudden blackouts were a common occurrence so, to enable the fixture to be fulfilled, Derby had connected the floodlights to a special emergency generator. When the game began it was Docherty's men who made the early running, pressurizing the Blues without creating too many clear-cut opportunities, and it was heartening for Gordon Lee to see Bob Latchford – watched again by England boss Ron Greenwood - and winger Dave Thomas prepared to fall back and defend when required. At the other end Colin Boulton made the save of the match from Jim Pearson's header.

Because of the unusual nature of the electricity supply there was always a chance that the ground could be plunged into darkness, and on 74 minutes that is exactly what happened. Like the United game two years before, the referee took the players from the pitch whilst officials hooked the lights back to the mains supply. The break took the steam out of Derby, and after 83 minutes Everton scored a winner that was undeserved, with Lyons heading forcefully home from a Ross free-kick. The Blues held on and the two points reinforced the view that they could be serious title challengers, but come the spring they would, in typical 70s style, come up just short.

There was one other oddity about this game; four players appeared in the two matches that were interrupted due to floodlight failure – Lyons, Dobson and Latchford for Everton and, remarkably, Gerry Daly who played in the midfield for both United in '75 and Derby County. Also, as you may have noticed, Tommy Docherty was in charge of the opposition on both occasions!

More Bonfire Night fireworks

Eighty-two years before the game at the Baseball Ground, Goodison Park staged its own pyrotechnics on November 5th, 1895. As an experiment the charity match between Everton and West Brom was played on that date in front of 16 specially provided Wells lights that were as 'light as day' according to the *Daily Post*, with the added bonus of a special firework display at the close. A total of 6,000 spectators braved the rain to see 'several fine set pieces' in the display that included some rather unusual effects: the recreation of Niagara Falls; fireworks that looked 'like a mechanical footballer' and the display finishing with fireworks that attempted to show the eruption of Mount Vesuvius.

'The new Johan Cruft'

Disaster at 'The Pawthorns'
West Bromwich Albion 3-0 Everton
First Division, 27th November, 1976

The author knows of two funny stories about West Brom. One concerns a sports quiz when the bemused team was asked: 'Who was the West Bromwich Albion featherweight champion between 1974-80?' The poor question master obviously did not realise that WBA in boxing parlance stands for World Boxing Association.

The other is a comically absurd incident at the Hawthorns. Late November 1976 was not a good time to be an Evertonian, the steady slide down the league following a 4-0 opening-day win at Loftus Road was causing concern. A 4-1 defeat at Newcastle three days before had set the alarm bells ringing, and also Dixie Dean's worsening health had resulted in the loss of a leg. Four days after this visit to the Midlands was a daunting League Cup tie at Manchester United.

Manager Billy Bingham was entering the last-chance saloon, and on the morning of the match he had flown to Brussels to secure the signature of one Duncan McKenzie. Steve Burtenshaw was in charge as the side visited the Midlands on a dismal November day. Terry Darracott returned, after asking Bingham to be dropped following some severe criticism from the crowd, whilst Mick Lyons partnered Bob Latchford in attack, which was normally a sign that things were not going as planned.

Albion had, unusually for the time, a player-manager in Johnny Giles. Making his home debut was David Cross, a bearded striker who had once netted after 15 seconds in a match at Goodison Park in 1973 for Norwich, and two years later would score a hat-trick on the opening day there for Coventry City.

The home team went ahead inside five minutes. Tony Brown was a regular scorer against Everton over the years, and he added another to his account when his brilliantly-timed run from midfield enabled him to run onto a Ray Treacy pass. Brown and Cross both went close until on 28 minutes came one of the craziest, most nonsensical episodes in an Everton game for many years.

Accounts vary about how an errant Jack Russell got onto the pitch, but everyone present agreed that the referee Mr Hunting - a not inappropriate name in a story when a dog is involved - was wrong when he allowed play to continue. The small white - or brown and white according to the very observant *Daily Mirror* - intruder chased the ball around the pitch for fully 60 seconds until it reached Ken McNaught, who lost control as the canine went for the ball (and him). The ball then arrived at the feet of Darracott, whose pass back to Dai Davies stopped short. The Everton keeper, who was clearly reticent to go near the ball when the dog was in close proximity, stayed rooted to his line. Full-back Dave Jones, meanwhile, stood motionless as he thought Davies was going for it, so David Cross took advantage of the indecision to dribble across the goal (and past the dog) to fire home. Our four-legged friend followed the ball into the net and promptly headed it. Although there were some complaints, the referee allowed the goal to stand. For the first time in Everton history a goal had been scored with a legitimate assist from a family pet.

Just before half-time Davies came out for a cross by Martin and missed the ball, enabling Treacy to ghost in and his header lobbed into the Everton net. The second half was much more even. Bob Latchford missed two easy chances whilst John Osborn saved well on two occasions from Andy King. However, little could be done to save a match that, in the *Daily Post's* words was 'about the tale of a good team, an indifferent team…and a dog.'

POSTSCRIPT:

There is only one place to start really. Referee John Hunting had little to say in his defence. "Cases like this have to be left to the referee's discretion, and I would have stopped the game straight away if I thought the dog was having a direct effect", he admitted before adding: "I thought by allowing the game to continue I was hoping the dog would go away of its own accord, but I can't argue from the Everton players' point of view."

Steve Burtenshaw was not amused: "I think the game should have been stopped because our players were definitely harassed by the dog." But the person who took the greatest umbrage at the defeat was John Moores, then Everton vice-chairman (although in reality he was still the de facto leader and therefore controlling force of the club). Moores had been at Blackpool looking at Mick Walsh (why?!) and had missed the game. The vice-chairman 'blew his top', according to Alex Goodman in the *Liverpool Echo* when he heard the result from the Hawthorns – what his reaction was to the news of a dog-assisted second goal is not known, unfortunately. "I am very disappointed with the current performance of Everton and our most devoted supporters feel the same way."

On the Monday, Moores dropped a bombshell: "I'm thinking of resigning." It was a reflection of the degree of personal responsibility he felt at the demise of the club (whether, at this point, John Carey ordered a taxi for the great man is unknown). Thankfully Moores did not carry through his threat, Dixie was to leave hospital, Duncan McKenzie finally signed and Everton won 3-0 at Old Trafford four days later. But Billy Bingham lost his job in January 1977.

Nevertheless the last word goes to John Roberts, the *Daily Express* journalist who was also writing the *Official Centenary History of Everton* at the time. Roberts ran an interview with the game's most important player – the Jack Russell. Well, a spoof interview anyway. Full of dreadful puns – apart from the one about The Pawthorns, which is the author's own 'work' – the chat covered the dog's desire to appear on 'Barkinson' as well as how: 'The new Johan Cruft will be adding some missing bite.'

Duncan McKenzie (above, left in picture) was signed soon after the shambles at The Hawthorns, although manager Billy Bingham (above, right in picture) did not last much longer in the Goodison hotseat

Déjà vu again

A match of multiple coincidences
Everton 5-0 Finn Harps
UEFA Cup first round, 26th September, 1978

When a side plays nearly 5,000 matches you would expect to see a few intriguing coincidences, and that is certainly the case with the Toffees. From the game featuring several unrelated players called Harris and the two penalties taken by T.E. Jones against the legendary Bert Trautmann (both described later in this section), fate has thrown up more than a fair share of oddities to suggest other forces were at work.

But one thing is for sure - no single pair of matches has thrown up a more varied set of interlinked events than the two legs of the UEFA Cup first round against the Irish side, Finn Harps, in 1978. The Irish team were European regulars during the decade, although their previous sojourn two seasons before had disastrous consequences – a 16-1 aggregate defeat to Derby County, including a 12-0 thrashing at the Baseball Ground.

The Blues had enjoyed a fine unbeaten start to the campaign and were a healthy second in the First Division. Having won the opening leg 5-0 in the Republic of Ireland, they were looking to build up a healthy aggregate total. The second match suffered by the fact the tie was over, and the game lacked that competitive edge required to make it an attractive spectacle. The *Liverpool Echo's* view of the return game was colourfully put '…take away the stands, the crowd, the pouring rain and we could have been back on the banks of the River Finn in County Donegal.'

The Blues did make inroads against a hard-working defence despite an excellent performance by Felix Healy, who would later play in the Football League and for Northern Ireland in the 1982 World Cup. There were some quality moments, not least a superb curling shot by Andy King from 20 yards that opened the scoring. Further goals came from a typically well-taken near-post header by Bob Latchford, and an easy third by Mick Walsh was followed by goals from Ross and then Dobson. Walsh's goal had a bit of comedy about it. The Finn Harps keeper slipped when collecting a back pass leaving him to walk the ball into the net, which was about the only piece of luck the striker had in front of goal in an unhappy spell at Goodison.

George Wood was a spectator at the other end, although he was called upon to make saves from Pat McGuinness and Logan. At the end of the game the Irish side was given a standing ovation by the Goodison faithful and left the pitch to the cheers of the Everton players.

So far nothing special you would say, although both legs were won 5-0, and it was also 2-0 at half-time in both games. But the patterns of the goals were also curiously similar, the second goal in each game was scored five minutes after the opener, with the third coming just after half-time and the fourth and fifth coming just after the hour mark in both matches.

But the strangest coincidence concerned the Finn Harps goalkeepers. Prior to the tie there had been only seven instances of an opposition keeper being replaced in Everton games, but in the first leg Joe Harper came on for Eddie Mahon, who had injured his back, and in the second match it was Harper's turn to injure his back, and Mahon took his place. Remarkable enough, but both substitutions took place in the 61st minute and on each occasion the first touch of the ball for the new keeper was to pick it out of the back of the net - with Bob Latchford scoring in Ireland and Martin Dobson at Goodison.

If that wasn't enough, then how about the Everton substitutions. Mark Higgins came on for Mick Lyons in the 68th minute in Donegal, and at Goodison, Higgins came on for Lyons...in the 68th minute.

Ten other Everton coincidences

1.   Our 3-2 victory at Portsmouth in April 1959 was the original commentator's nightmare as there were four players, all unrelated, called Harris – Jimmy and Brian Harris lined up for the Blues whilst Pompey had Peter and Harry Harris. Our next game saw Jimmy and Brian line-up against Gerry Harris of Wolves. Jimmy and Brian are the pair of players with the same surname who have played for Everton on the most occasions, 138 matches after coincidentally both making their debut against Burnley in August 1955 (for a further Harris coincidence, see the Tottenham game of 1958).

2.   When Everton and Liverpool played their FA Cup third-round ties at home on January 7th 1956, the respective referees bizarrely lived in the same

street in Nottingham and a linesman at Goodison was called Mr Nottingham!

3.   Everyone is familiar with the fact that Dixie Dean scored his 60th league goal of the 1927-28 season against Arsenal, but less well known is that the Gunners were the opposition in a number of other landmark games in the great man's career. Dixie made his Everton debut at Highbury in March 1925 and on the opening day of the season in 1936-37 he equalled Steve Bloomer's league record of 352 goals on the same ground, when the referee was 'Lol' Harper, who was in charge in the famous game in 1928. He scored the final goal of his Everton career at Goodison against Arsenal on the opening day of the season 12 months later.

4.   Steve Watson is the last Everton player whose final goals for the club were actually part of a hat-trick – netting three against Leeds United in a 4-0 home victory in September 2003. The last Everton player prior to Watson whose final goals were also a hat-trick was Robert 'Bunny' Bell in October 1938. These also came in a 4-0 home win over Leeds and, like the Geordie, he completed his hat-trick in the 52nd minute.

5.   The successful penalty taken by T.E. Jones for the Blues scored past Manchester City's Bert Trautmann in January 1959 was not the first taken by the defender against the legendary keeper - he had scored a penalty against the German as a junior during a friendly match when Trautmann had been a prisoner-of-war.

6.   When Everton won the FA Cup in 1906 they had a Sharp, Scott and Young in the side; when they won the trophy in 1966 they had a Scott and a Young and in 1984 they had a Sharp. Indeed, Alex 'Sandy' Young (1906) and Alex Young (1966) provide the only instance of exact namesakes winning FA Cup winner's medals with the same club.

7.   The League Cup tie against Chelsea at Stamford Bridge in October 1985 was the first time both sides had scored in the opening two minutes of an Everton match, with Kerry Dixon scoring after 53 seconds and Kevin Sheedy replying straight from the kick-off. This has happened on only one occasion since, remarkably in the Toffees' next away game in that competition, at Newport County 12 months later.

8.   Everton winger Tommy Ring was marked by full-back Bobby Bell of Newcastle in a 1959 league match at St James' Park. Other aptly-named opponents include Barry Horne and Gary Bull of Nottingham Forest (1995), and (Gerry) Sweeney and (Colin) Todd were the right-backs when Bristol City played Everton in September 1978.

9.   On 31st January 1931 Everton recorded their biggest away win of the century in the FA Cup – 6-0 at Selhust Park against Crystal Palace. On 21st January 1939 Everton equalled their biggest home win of the century in the competition, winning 8-0 against Doncaster Rovers. Remarkably the same keeper was on the receiving end on both occasions, James Imrie.

10.   Ball, Harvey and Kendall were playing in the same match for the first time in many years in 2002, but it wasn't on the football pitch. The limited-overs game between Hampshire and Gloucestershire saw Will Kendall face Martyn Ball and Ian Harvey.

On another cricket point, Sir Everton Weekes, the great West Indian batsman of the 1940s and 50s, was interviewed by Peter West on the BBC in 1976, and he revealed his christian name came from his father, who was an Everton fan, as they were one of the biggest clubs in England. In his honour many West Indians born in Weekes' era on the pitch were also christened Everton, for example three of their Test XI against England in 1981: the batsman Everton Matthis and the fearsome bowlers Andy Roberts and Colin Croft, who both had Everton as a middle name. Some footballers have also had Everton in their name, most notoriously the one-time Liverpool winger, Mark Everton Walters, who very nearly joined the Blues from Aston Villa in the late 80s.

Tommy Ring (above right), part of an Everton coincidence

A bet, a brawl and a stranger baring all

'A game that had everything'
Liverpool 2-2 Everton
First Division, 20th October, 1979

Merseyside derby matches of the late 70s/early 80s could be heartless, soulless affairs both on and off the pitch. There was certainly a sinister atmosphere to the games at that time and the bad feeling resulted in the career-ending challenge on Geoff Nulty of Everton at Goodison in March 1980 - the game unfortunately best remembered for the death of Dixie Dean after a heart attack.

But the Anfield derby in 1979-80 was memorable for other, contrasting reasons. Indeed, it is certainly the leading candidate for the craziest, most bizarre encounter of the 200 or so between the city's two clubs since the first in 1894. The *Daily Mirror* maintained that: 'The match was loaded with incident, but it was one which any resemblance to football was purely coincidental.'

Liverpool had made an uncharacteristically hesitant start to the campaign whilst Everton's win against Crystal Palace the previous week was only their fifth in 23 league matches since March. Martin Dobson and Dave Thomas had left during the summer and newcomers Garry Stanley, Brian Kidd and John Bailey had found it difficult to bed into a side struggling for confidence.

The day itself was bright and perfect for football as Phil Thompson and then Mick Lyons led out their respective teams to a capacity crowd. As you would expect Liverpool had all the early pressure and penned the Toffees back into their own area. It was then after eight minutes, from nothing, that the Reds went ahead. A long ball down the middle from Alan Kennedy was headed down by centre-half Mark Higgins to Lyons, under no pressure, beautifully lobbed the ball over George Wood from 25 yards out at the Anfield Road End. A television strike ensured that Mick's misfortune is not captured for posterity, but a well-known tale was that one Toffees fan that night was happy, as Lyons would later memorably recall:

"I was still feeling rotten when I went out with some of the lads for a drink after the match. There was an Evertonian in the pub, who was going on and on to me (about) what a great player I was. After Andy King asked him to leave me alone because I was so down, he turns round and said that he was actually made up with me, as he'd won £40 on me in the sweep to score the first goal."

Although the Blues tried to get a foothold in the match, it was all Liverpool in the aftermath of Lyons' strike, but after 14 minutes the visitors unexpectedly levelled. A free-kick by Wright was headed away by Hansen and when Ross returned the ball into the middle, Brian Kidd, on his derby debut, took advantage of indecision between Thompson and Clemence to head home. Souness was then booked for a foul on King, as Everton were now enjoying their best spell of the match, using the long ball for Bob Latchford's head to good effect, although chances were scarce.

In the lead-up to half-time, though, Liverpool regained the ascendancy with both Dalglish and McDermott firing wide when well placed. They then saw their best chance to take the lead, with McDermott forcing a fine save from Wood after a delicate chip from Souness.

It was McDermott again who caused Everton a scare straight from the kick-off in the second half when the midfielder's first-time shot struck the base of Wood's right-hand post. The Everton keeper, not for the first time at Anfield, was having a superb game – he had almost single-handedly denied the Reds a win seven months previously in a 1-1 draw - and he was called upon again to save bravely at the feet of Alan Kennedy, after a perfect through ball by Dalglish. Feeling the pressure, Everton now had a nine-man defence and eventually they were broken with a fine goal by Ray Kennedy, who found space on the left after a neat flick-on by Dalglish, before shooting past Wood in front of an ecstatic Kop. The Scottish keeper was then called upon to make further saves from McDermott and Alan Kennedy as Liverpool dominated. It was to be an hour before Everton got their first corner, with Lyons heading over.

After Dalglish had missed the best chance of the game by firing wide after being put clean through, Everton again found an equalizer against the run of play after 67 minutes. Great work by Kidd took him past the Liverpool defence and his weighted pass fed King, who beat Clemence with a well-placed strike into the corner of the net. It was the third consecutive derby match in which the effervescent midfielder had struck.

Three minutes later came the second famous incident of this memorable game. A bad foul by Stanley on Johnson about 10 yards outside of the area resulted in a 20-man brawl in front of the Kop. Although many punches were thrown, it was McDermott and Stanley who were singled out for attention by the referee, Mr Richardson, and given their marching orders.

The irony was that, out of the 20 outfield players, Stanley and McDermott would probably have been last on the list of those you would have expected to see dismissed, with the added incongruity that they were actually drinking partners as well. For 25 years they were regarded as the first dismissals in Merseyside derby matches, but subsequent research by the author indicated that this was not the case (see Postscript).

The game had now become frenzied and Everton found themselves, not for the first time, trapped in their penalty box. Wood made another great save from Ray Kennedy and they survived a penalty appeal when Ross brought down Dalglish. Before the end of the encounter, though, came the third and final reason why this match has passed into derby folklore. Gordon Lee takes up the story:

"Jimmy McGregor (the Everton physio) keeps nudging me. 'Look at this.' But I can't see anything. He keeps digging me, saying: 'Look at this, look at this.' And then I see the two policemen bringing the streaker round the ground." (Gordon's subsequent alleged comments to Jim McGregor unfortunately cannot be included!)

The streaker was wearing a sweater, and nothing else except for an Everton scarf around her neck, and had invaded the playing area to the amusement of the crowd. Eventually the lady, Eileen Finnan, was escorted off the pitch with a strategically-placed cape ensuring no further embarrassment was caused. The *Daily Mirror's* view was quite clear though. 'She could hardly be described as bottomless because that part of her anatomy wobbled most charmingly', before adding that she 'gave Ray Clemence a better close-up than he had of the two Everton goals.' But this was not the last time Ms Finnan would make the headlines.

Although Liverpool continued to press, the Blues steadfastly refused to capitulate and soon after Mr Richardson blew the final whistle, after what had been a breathless match full of the weird and wonderful.

POSTSCRIPT:

The *Daily Express* asserted that the game was: 'One of the most amazing confrontations between the red and blue of Merseyside.' Garry Stanley - signed for £300,000 in the summer - was adamant that he had the rough end of the stick. "I think I was a victim of circumstances. I have never been sent off before in my life and I can honestly say I didn't throw any punches", before adding that "I went to see the referee after the game and he said 'do yourself a favour and go away'."

His drinking partner Terry McDermott remained tight-lipped, but Jimmy Case gave an insight into the punch-up: "I can remember going in for the ball and finishing up on the floor. David Johnson was on the floor and I think it was Garry Stanley throwing punches." The referee Mr Richardson quite wisely decided to lock himself in the dressing room for an hour afterwards.

In 2004 it was established by the author that the famous joint sending-off in this game was not the first time players had been ordered from the pitch in the Merseyside derby, as had been reported both at the time and in subsequent record books. In 1896 Alfred Milward of Everton (one of the club's stars of the 19th century) was dismissed for foul play in the goalless draw at Anfield.

Meanwhile in the week following the match it was alleged that Ms Finnan was the member of a religious cult, and she was soon back on the front pages of the local press when she disappeared soon after the game, and then had to be rescued safely from the River Mersey, three days later, after jumping into the river. She thankfully survived.

A couple of odd stoppages

Spurs at Wembley, Aston Villa, 12th March 1977

Such was the passive nature of the League Cup final, that when the referee called the players together in the middle of the pitch after 51 minutes, some observers remarked that it was probably to ask for a bit more in the way of positive play. The stoppage was because the referee had found a pair of spurs belonging to a member of the band who had been on the pitch at half-time, so for several minutes everyone fruitlessly checked to see if there were any more.

Paolo stops game, West Ham, 16th December 2000

Probably the most famous case of player intervention at Goodison. As the game reached injury time, Paul Gerrard was injured when challenging for the ball on the far left-hand side of the area. When the ball was returned to the centre of the box, di Canio sportingly caught the ball to stop play. He got a round of applause from the Gwladys Street End, but what Harry Redknapp really thought may have been different.

Derby action, 1979. Top: The 20-man brawl in full swing. Above left: Streaker Eileen Finnan is led off the pitch. Above, right (top): George Wood lies flat-out on the Anfield turf. Above, right (bottom): Terry McDermott sees red

MOMENTS

Above: 'Goodison Park's strange interlude arrived when a spectator encroached on the pitch and got among the Preston North End players. He was chased by a constable and by Else, the Preston goalkeeper, out of whose grip he struggled. Later, the Preston half-back (Tommy) Docherty collared him after a rugby tackle. Neither club would bring charges against the man.' (Taken from original newspaper cutting, 1958)

Above: 'Play stops at Stamford Bridge while the referee restores order. Mr J.W. Hunt, with his hand on the shoulder of Blunstone (Chelsea), beckons to other players. On the left are Collins and Jones (Everton) with Brabrook (Chelsea) and Laverick (Everton) wraps his arms round Greaves (Chelsea).'
Below: 'Laverick (Everton) at grips with a spectator, who has run on to the field, with police hurrying to lend a hand. The referee is busy with a group of players from both sides' (text taken from original Liverpool Daily Post & Echo cuttings, 1959). Incidentally the pictures taken were following a run-in between Collins and Blunstone (above), with the below picture showing Laverick dealing with a pitch invader

Above: An Everton penalty appeal is turned down, to the anguish of Ray Wilson (No 3). Alan Ball (second left) would be sent off for his protests soon after, 1968

Below left and right: 'Banks does not seem at all happy.' Victoria Ground, Stoke, 1968. The goal post threatens to collapse after players had crashed into it, Stoke v Everton

'Above: 'The kick-off at Goodison Park this afternoon was delayed for five minutes while several of the Southampton players changed their boots after testing the frost-covered pitch.' Taken from original cutting, December 14, 1968 - note a young Mick Channon in the right of the picture

Above: Joe Royle (No 9) and Alan Ball (partially hidden, seventh left) are surrounded by youngsters delighted with a goal in the League Cup against Tranmere Rovers, September 1968.

Below: Referee Pat Partridge (Middlesbrough) gives a free-kick to Blackpool, rather than a third goal for Everton's Colin Harvey, with the disbelieving Joe Royle being adjudged to have impeded the goalkeeper. According to the original cutting, '...the joy of the boys is short-lived'

Above: Everton trial game (firsts v reserves). August 1967, and Mike Trebilcock chips the ball over Gordon West to give his side the lead. For the record, the annual match was discontinued in 1970.

Above: December 1975, and one of five goals to fly past Birmingham City goalkeeper Dave Latchford - brother of Everton legend Bob. However, the main interest for the writer of the original cutting was in the weather-beaten 'Please refrain from throwing missiles' hoarding, which appears to resemble a Russian slogan. 'OH VOT A GOAL, GOAL, GOAL!' ran the original headline.

Below: Everton v Home Farm, pre-season friendly 1976, with the Irish side sporting Everton's away strip

Above: Jubilant Dukla Prague fans wave a banner as Everton slide out of the UEFA Cup in 1978 - just a shame they had the wrong club...

Above: Eamonn O'Keefe's boot connects with a Crystal Palace player, 1981.
Below: Gary Stevens on target for Everton at Birmingham, sporting the home side's away shirts, 1984

Above: A lone supporter watches on as Wimbledon v Everton attracts a post-War top-flight low of 3,039 spectators, January 1993.
Below: The red-carded Neville Southall is replaced at Sheffield Wednesday by reserve goalkeeper Jason Kearton at Sheffield Wednesday, February 1993

Drama at the Vicarage

'Everton stage a remarkable comeback'
Watford 4-4 Everton
First Division, 25th February, 1984

What marks this match out as unusual is not so much the scoreline - although eight-goal thrillers hardly grow on trees - more so that at 1-0 to the home side against an off-colour Everton, just before the hour mark on a miserable February afternoon, the bookmakers would have given long-odds on the game veering out of control so spectacularly.

Everton were in the middle of a splendid run of results – the second half of the season would see the club display championship-winning form as well as reaching two cup finals. Howard Kendall, though, would spring a surprise before the game by dropping Andy King for Andy Gray in attack. The Hornets were also in good nick, having enjoyed an equally fruitful post-Christmas period, which had seen them climb out of the relegation zone and, in John Barnes and Maurice Johnston, they had two of the country's form players. Johnston, in fact, had been looked at closely by the Blues boss before Graham Taylor signed him. Kendall would get his man seven years later, but the sharpness and clinical finishing that had set the league alight in the mid-1980s was sadly a thing of the past.

It was Barnes who made the first impression, dangerously raiding down the right and his resulting cross was well saved by Southall as Johnston lingered dangerously. Nigel Callaghan shot wide when well placed and then the Welsh keeper required two attempts to clear the ball as Barnes raced onto a through pass. It was also the future England winger's shot that led to a fine Southall save on 24 minutes, although from the resulting corner the same player got a head to Callaghan's cross to give Watford a thoroughly deserved lead. Little had been seen of the Blues' attack during the first half and frustration took its toll as first Stevens, and then Mountfield and Ratcliffe, were spoken to by referee Vic Callow for fouls. One national daily was particularly critical: 'For the first 45 minutes Everton were hopeless. Watching Everton play away over the years has sometimes been as enjoyable as toothache.'

The start of the second half would see a similar pattern, with Watford pressurising the Blues at every turn. But the visitors started to see more of the ball, and after 52 minutes Sharp clinically dispatched a volley home in typical style after good work from Reid. However, the equality would be short-lived. Five minutes later Johnston restored Watford's lead with a header, for his 17th goal in 20 matches, after a huge throw-in by centre-half Steve Sims caused confusion in the Blues' defence. In the 64th minute the match seemed over: a disastrous back pass from Stevens went straight to Barnes, who beat Southall easily.

But amazingly the Blues refused to lie down. Alan Irvine immediately had two chances to close the gap but his first-time volley was well saved by Sherwood and then he shot just over after cutting inside from the right flank. But the pressure brought its just rewards when just three minutes after Watford's third, Sheedy's cross from the right was arrowed past keeper Steve Sherwood by the head of Andy Gray – not for the last time that season, as it transpired.

A game that was meandering nowhere just 15 minutes earlier had now generated a life of its own, as both sides pressed for goals. As the away team pushed forward there were gaps at the back and with a quarter of an hour remaining the Hornets restored their two-goal advantage, when a Callaghan corner again caused confusion in the Everton defence, and full-back Wilf Rostron – who would later be suspended for the FA Cup final - nipped in to score. But the Blues were still not finished, and after more sustained pressure Graeme Sharp pulled a goal back by deftly sidestepping Franklin and beating Sherwood with only 11 minutes left. Cue a frantic finale with chances to both teams and amazingly with the match in injury time, Adrian Heath fired in from the edge of the box. The reaction of the Everton players said it all, each outfielder piled on top of 'Inchy' in a manner not too dissimilar to the Goodison derby goal celebrations 20 years later.

Howard Kendall was not impressed after the game though: "When we were 3-2 down I thought we were going to win but another silly goal meant the best we could hope for was a draw." But what a second half it had been, seven goals, chances at both ends and Everton showing a resilience that would typify their mid-80s revival.

POSTSCRIPT:

Such was the high-octane entertainment provided in the second half that the *Daily Express* prophetically informed readers that 'if Watford and Everton reach Wembley then stick to your television sets, even if the first half is a bit dull.' Both teams would of course play in the Cup final and the Blues, after some scary moments along the way, would eventually triumph 2-0. In fact the first half was a bit dull for the neutral and so too was the second – but who really cared?

In September 1984 there was an even higher-scoring match at Vicarage Road in the next league meeting - Everton winning 5-4, but it was about as ordinary as nine-goal thrillers get and despite the scoreline it failed to match the rather unexpected storyline of this encounter.

Richo's odd shirt

Watch the 1984 FA Cup final again and one Everton player is different from the rest. Kevin Richardson had injured his arm in the League Cup semi-final and his plaster-cast was deemed unsafe to wear with the bespoke short-sleeved blue shirts for the final, which had been embroidered with the match details. Richo had to make do with the standard home shirt from the season.

Despite the look of disgust, Graeme Sharp (right) has pulled the score back to 4-3

'We paid good money for this Kendall'

End-of-season farce at Luton
Luton Town 2-0 Everton
First Division, 28th May, 1985

The final game of the momentous 1984-85 campaign ended in farcical circumstances when the Blues were forced to field a severely weakened team, which was stripped of players through injury or international duty.

With four players in the England squad (Stevens, Steven, Reid and Bracewell) and two players with Scotland (Andy Gray and Graeme Sharp, who both played up-front in Iceland on the same night) plus Kevin Sheedy with the Republic of Ireland, the 11,000 Luton fans who were seeking revenge against their FA Cup semi-final conquerors were to be sorely disappointed. Add in the fact that Derek Mountfield and Ian Atkins were both injured, and it was no surprise that manager Howard Kendall was verbally abused at Kenilworth Road before the game by opposition fans. "You're a disgrace, we paid good money for this Kendall," said one disillusioned customer behind the dugout. "I know you did, I did try but it isn't our fault," replied the Blues boss.

The line-up did have a strange look to say the least. Although Neville Southall – who was captain for the first time – Pat Van den Hauwe, Kevin Richardson and John Bailey were in the team, others were not so familiar: Darren Hughes, Johnny Morrissey Junior and Rob Wakenshaw had only featured in a handful of matches previously, plus it was to be the only game in the Everton careers of Jason Danskin, Derek Walsh and Neill Rimmer. The average age of the team was 21 years, six months, which is second only to the side fielded at Leeds in April 1966.

Ironically Hughes, Morrissey and Wakenshaw may not have been there in the first place. In September 1984 they had been in an Everton reserve side that had lost 6-2 at Sheffield United, having been leading 2-0 at half-time. All three players, plus Stuart Rimmer (who was later to become Chester City's all-time leading scorer) and Ian Bishop (who was to have a long and distinguished career with West Ham and was still playing in the Premiership in 2001 with Manchester City) were transfer-listed by the Blues boss, as on the night at Bramall Lane: "In a number of young players, I did not see the attitude which would have put things right."

The game itself was a typically lethargic end-of-season affair, with the mood of the home fans hardly enhanced by a slick offside trap employed by the champions which the Blues manager defended – "It's up to teams to find a way past it." The Luton fans showed their appreciation by slow handclapping whenever a home player was caught out. Meka Nwajobi put the Hatters ahead after three minutes from a Harford cross and just before the hour Ricky Hill headed past the stranded Neville Southall via a Peter Nicholas centre. Everton in reply had one opportunity, a shot from Paul Wilkinson – another with only a handful of games - that hit the post.

And that was that. Strange that such a momentous season should end up in such curious circumstances but it was also appropriate that Footballer of the Year Neville Southall was awarded the man-of-the-match award in the *Liverpool Echo*, on the basis that 'he had tried harder than most to play as though the game was important.' As for Danskin, Walsh et al, then their appearances are merely a footnote in the season's record. But at least they could say they played in a Championship-winning team!

POSTSCRIPT:

The *Daily Mirror* had the knives out for the Blues boss after the game, especially over his game plan: 'Everton Football Club should dig deep into the profits they have made this season and give a refund to the fans who turned up at Kenilworth Road. The absences should not excuse the negative tactics they took into a match with nothing at stake.' Howard had the last word though: "I was proud of my kids."

The victorious 1984 FA Youth Cup-winning team, some of whom would appear at Kenilworth Road

Whatever happened to?

Darren Hughes

After scoring in the 1984 FA Youth Cup final win, this was the third and final game of the full-back's Everton career. He joined Shrewsbury a month after – recording an unfortunate own goal in the Toffees' 4-1 League Cup win there later in the year - and then later played in over 200 games for Port Vale.

Johnny Morrissey (Junior)

Son of the 1960s winger, this was his only first-team start but he would later become a Tranmere stalwart, playing for over 14 years at Prenton Park.

Robbie Wakenshaw

A prolific scorer at youth and reserve level – earlier that season he had netted six goals in a Central League match at Bradford – the blonde-haired striker was, like the equally prolific Tony McLoughlin 20 years before, denied opportunities at Goodison due to the strength of the squad. He was also the only Everton player to admit a fondness for the music of Olivia Newton John in the match programme, which may have influenced his first-team chances. He played for several lower league teams before his career ended in 1988. Last heard of as a welder.

Jason Danskin

The midfielder stayed at Goodison until 1987, but failed to make another first-team appearance despite being made substitute on a couple of occasions.

Derek Walsh

The only appearance of this Scottish utility player's Everton career. He would later play for Hamilton Academical with David Moyes. Last heard of as a plumber in Carlisle.

Neill Rimmer

A fine player at schoolboy level for England, this was the midfielder's sole Everton game – a 15-minute cameo as a substitute. Later played for Ipswich and Wigan.

Leeds United – April 1966 (a)

An even younger side played in the 4-1 defeat at Leeds United in April 1966, when Harry Catterick rested several players in advance of the FA Cup semi-final and received a £2,000 fine from the FA for his trouble. Joe Royle was the baby of the team, having just turned 17, but there were five other teenagers (Frank Darcy, John Hurst, Gerry Glover, Jimmy Husband, Derek Smith) plus Gerry Humphreys (20), Andy Rankin (21), Mike Trebilcock (21), Johnny Morrissey (25) and Sandy Brown (27). The average age of the side was just 20 years, 11 months.

Everton's youth team, pictured in July 1965 with the FA Youth Cup. Back row left to right: Ron Lewin (coach), David Pearson, Dennis Yaager, Frank Darcy, Geoff Barnett, John Hurst, David Grant, Harry Catterick (first-team manager).
Front row left to right: Alec Wallace, Gerry Glover, Eric Curwen (captain), Tony McLoughlin, Jimmy Husband, Aiden Maher.
Five of the players were included in the first team in the infamous 4-1 defeat at Leeds United in April the following year.

Southall sensation

'Incident-packed is hardly the phrase for this game'
Chelsea 2-1 Everton
First Division, 12th October, 1985

G oals (two in a minute), missed penalties from both teams, three goalkeepers from the same international side, two centre-forwards vying for international recognition and 10 men heroically trying to save the game were the features of this extraordinary encounter at Stamford Bridge on a beautiful autumnal afternoon in the mid-1980s.

The Blues travelled to the Bridge having made an uncertain start to the defence of their title. In fact they stood 11 points behind a rampant Manchester United, who had won 10 and drew one of their opening 11 matches. This was the period when 'Give it to them now' was a regular headline across the national press, as they gushed over the spectacular start made by Ron Atkinson's team (it was to soon end in tears as Merseyside's big two ensured that United famously finished fourth in what had been described as a one-horse race). Meanwhile Chelsea were confirming their promise of the previous season, and at the start of the day they stood one point ahead of the Blues. It was a fine side – the powerful strike force of Kerry Dixon and David Speedie complemented by the trickery of Pat Nevin and the midfield drive of Nigel Spackman, whilst in goal they had Eddie Niedzwiecki, understudy to Neville Southall at international level.

Everton were a goal down inside four minutes, as a throw-in the left saw Speedie break free and his fine cross was converted ruthlessly by Dixon with a bullet-header, in the presence of England boss Bobby Robson. As strange as it seems now, at the time the Chelsea striker and his opposite number on the Everton side that day, Gary Lineker, were seen as the two main rivals for the vacant England No 9 shirt. But a hat-trick by the former Leicester striker against Turkey the following week would make his claim indisputable and the rest, as they say, is history.

Chelsea continued to dominate and, with the visitors' defence clearly rattled, it was no surprise that on 20 minutes they were awarded a penalty, when Speedie raced clear of the defence and was brought down by Southall as he took the ball around the advancing keeper. Nowadays such an offence would lead to an instant red card but the only punishment was a booking as the Welshman – ironically described as 'quiet and undemonstrative' in the match programme - disputed the award. There was a real let-off though for Everton as Spackman, a replacement taker for Dixon who had missed during the week, hammered the kick high over the bar. Two chances immediately followed with Speedie again firing wide when he went clear and Graeme Sharp missing the visitors' first opportunity when glancing a header wide.

There was more excitement in the five minutes before half-time. First Chelsea went two goals up after Nevin had tricked his way past Bailey on the Everton left and Speedie nodded the cross past a helpless Southall. Within 60 seconds the Toffees pulled one back when Bracewell fed Sheedy at the edge of the Chelsea box and that famous left foot did the rest.

On the resumption Everton, clearly buoyed by their unexpected strike, enjoyed their best spell of the match culminating in the award of a penalty for a foul on Trevor Steven by that rugged Scottish centre-half Doug Rougvie. (The Chelsea defender was once memorably described by one critic as being about 'as mobile as a telegraph pole, but far less reliable.') Graeme Sharp took the kick but he, like Spackman before him, missed the target, this time firing wide of the right-hand post. It was only the second time in a post-War game involving Everton in the top-flight that both teams had missed penalties; the previous occurrence had been just six months before, at Old Trafford when Strachan and Sheedy missed in a 1-1 draw.

Seven minutes later came the game's most controversial incident. A long ball pumped forward by Speedie was left for Dixon to chase but Southall raced off his line and in a purely reflex action, from a position of some 15 yards outside of the box, caught the ball above his head. There was no immediate reaction by the Everton staff until they realised the great Welshman had been booked in the first half, leaving referee Vic Callow no option but to send Southall off. It was only the second dismissal in history of an Everton keeper and as Southall left the pitch he threw his shirt down in disgust, then threw his gloves at the referee and brushed aside a member of the Everton bench before entering the tunnel – although this appeared to be in total frustration over his own mistake than the official's judgement. His skipper for both club and country, Kevin Ratcliffe, took over in goal. The centre-half was the third player from the same international team to play in goal in the game, surely some sort of record.

Ratcliffe more than held his own to be fair, diving to his left to keep out a Speedie drive and saving one-handed from a Hazard chip. It was at the other end where the real pressure was applied, with Niedzwiecki saving well on three occasions as Everton gave more credence to the theory about 10 men being harder to beat than a full side. But try as they might, the Blues failed to grab an unlikely equaliser, leaving Chelsea with the three points and a 27,000 crowd with an afternoon they would never forget.

POSTSCRIPT:

The Everton keeper remained largely silent after the match – "It was a moment of daft amnesia" was his only quote - but he had an unlikely ally in the aftermath of this memorable match: his close friend and international team-mate Eddie Niedzweicki. "I know how Neville feels. I was sent off for the same offence recently. The ball bounced up and he's a professional. He doesn't like to let goals in." The Chelsea keeper also spoke about Southall's feelings over his initial booking: "Neville feels he didn't touch anybody." Howard Kendall took a more pragmatic view: "The referee was 100% right. Neville made two bad decisions and now he regrets them."

This was not the only controversial game between the two sides at the Bridge that season. Six weeks later a League Cup tie between the teams was just as memorable. Both sides scored in the first two minutes (Dixon for Chelsea and Sheedy for the Toffees) before Bracewell put the Blues ahead after just 12 minutes. The shape of the game changed following Sheedy's dismissal for what is known in the trade as 'foul and industrial' language. Nevin equalised in the second half for Chelsea and the Londoners went on to win an equally bad-tempered replay, when Darren Wood would become the third player dismissed between the teams that season.

If Everton did have a bogey side in the mid-80s glory years then the London club were it. They were the only club who avoided defeat at Goodison in the two championship-winning seasons and during 1985-86 the Toffees drew a blank in four meetings both home and away.

Everton outfielders as keepers: a brief history

Kevin Ratcliffe was the last in the increasingly dying breed of outfield players appearing as a substitute keeper for the Toffees. More than a few have been required to do this over the years, going back to the three keepers at Sheffield United in 1895 (see Match 2) and then David Storrier replacing the injured 'Rab' McFarlane for 10 minutes in the first half at Derby County in September 1897 (ironically when Storrier returned to his normal left-back berth for the second period he was carried-off injured himself).

After Storrier in 1897 there were intermittent sightings of outfielders in goal, such as full-back Jack Crelley for Billy Scott at Sheffield United in October 1905 and defender John Maconnachie for Tom Fern at Burnley in April 1914. In the inter-War years there were several other instances, most notably the two separate appearances of another full-back, John O'Donnell, at St. Andrew's against Birmingham in September 1925 and January 1928 – the latter was memorable for the fact that during a tenure in between the sticks of no more than 60 seconds the opposition managed to score. Defenders Dicky Downs, Tom Fleetwood, Warney Cresswell and forward 'Bunny' Bell (for Ted Sagar against Leicester in 1937, described at Match 20) all had a go in this period.

The post-War years did not see many outfielders in the keeper's jersey. Brian Harris at Blackburn in 1962 replaced Albert Dunlop and Sandy Brown donned the green shirt on a couple of memorable occasions described elsewhere. Between those two and Kevin Ratcliffe, the only outfielder to go in goal was Mr Versatility himself – Mick Lyons. The 1970s stalwart did so in April 1973 against West Brom in place of David Lawson (when he conceded two goals, making him the last outfielder to concede a goal, on the day Harry Catterick was effectively relieved of his managerial duties) and then in April 1982 he replaced Neville Southall, who was taken off with concussion, for the final moments of the match against Manchester United at Goodison. It was his final bow as an Everton player on the ground.

There have been even fewer occasions when the opposition have been required to do so. Julian Dicks of West Ham went in goal after the dismissal of Ludek Miklosko at Goodison in December 1995, and was immediately beaten by David Unsworth from the spot. Three months earlier Dicks had netted from the spot at Upton Park against the Toffees, so he can claim a unique double: both scoring and facing penalties against Everton.

But perhaps the most unfortunate case of substitute goalkeeping was by Terry Jones in a FA Youth Cup game for the Blues against Preston North End in December 1992. Having put Everton 2-1 up with a 35-yard screamer and a free-kick, he took over in goal when goalkeeper Stephen Reeves was sent off four minutes from time for a foul in the area. Jones failed to stop the resulting penalty-kick and then conceded the winner after a defensive mix-up. His contribution to the game was scored two, conceded two.

Disbelief for skipper Kevin Ratcliffe, who comes off at Stamford Bridge having kept a clean sheet against Chelsea as Neville Southall's replacement

'Rumour man' has a field day

An afternoon of mixed emotions
Everton 6-1 Southampton
First Division, 3rd May, 1986

The 1985-86 season was a strange campaign. As gates sank to a post-War low, the absence of TV cameras before Christmas lent an air of mystery to proceedings (that season's scoring sensation, West Ham United's Frank McAvennie, was largely unknown to those outside of the East End until the New Year). The classic derby match against Liverpool at Goodison in September could be seen abroad, but not here.

The Blues would eventually finish as runners-up in both major domestic competitions, despite a crippling injury list that meant at any given point in the season they were usually deprived of at least one of their championship-winning midfield quartet of Reid, Bracewell, Sheedy and Steven. (Indeed they all appeared together in only six matches in all during 1985-86 which, considering Everton only lost five of the 50 games in total they played together for the club, indicates that had they been available for the whole campaign then the Blues probably would have retained the title with some ease.) Throw in the absence of Neville Southall from the end of March and it is a wonder how they got so close.

By the time of the final league weekend of the season there were three teams still in the running - the two Merseyside giants and West Ham, who were enjoying their best-ever campaign:

Liverpool	85 pts, 41 games
West Ham	81 pts, 40 games
Everton	80 pts, 40 games

Liverpool played at Chelsea whilst West Ham visited West Brom. The possible scenarios have been painfully covered many times, but an inferior goal difference meant an Everton win against the Saints was needed, at least to stay in the contest. The Blues, rather unusually, had a slice of luck on the eve of the game. The south-coast side were deprived of Peter Shilton and key defenders Mark Wright, Kevin Bond and Mark Dennis, all through injury. Their absence was covered by, amongst others, a 17-year-old keeper who had not even turned out for the reserves (Keith Grainger) and a 16-year-old defender in Allen Tankard.

The match started in an atmosphere that can best be described as 'optimism mixed with a fair degree of pessimism.' The home side were confident of victory and supporters were mindful that Chelsea had until recently been in the title hunt themselves. In contrast Liverpool were on a roll and had won at the Bridge in the FA Cup in January. The Everton manager summed it up: "Let's just say I'm a Chelsea fan now." But some fans obviously knew the writing was on the wall, as the crowd of 33,000 was substantially down on the two previous home fixtures.

Everton had also quite literally lost their shooting boots at the crucial time. The previous nine league games had seen them net on just seven occasions. The free-scoring Gary Lineker especially was enjoying (if that's the word) a goal drought. Three days before his lucky footwear had famously gone AWOL and the replacements failed to do the forward justice at Oxford.

But this day, with the pressure slightly less intense and against a makeshift back-line, it was clear that the goal-happy days of earlier had returned. As a matter of fact it took only 10 minutes for the floodgates to open, the goalkeeper flapping at a free-kick and letting Mountfield pounce from close range. After 29 minutes Lineker turned provider with a fine cross that Steven glanced perfectly past the rookie keeper. Enter 'Rumour Man.'

'Rumour Man' was a mythical beast who roamed the Goodison Park terraces and was a source of much disinformation on key matchdays, especially during the mid-80s, and this was without a doubt his finest hour. With Liverpool needing to lose, stories abounded within the ground that Chelsea had gone ahead (in fact several 'Rumour Men' were at work on this day as, from the Main Stand, many different pockets of supporters could be seen at any one-time celebrating). By the time of the second goal the crowd was in a state of what can only be described as collective hyperventilation - a condition made worse by the sight of Lineker poaching a typical third a minute or so after Steven's effort.

After 34 minutes it was now 4-0 with Bracewell threading a typically accurate through ball for Lineker to score goal 36 for the season from about 12 yards. Such was the interest of events elsewhere that the goal was met with a degree of indifference, but between then and half-time the reality of the situation hit home: Liverpool were actually leading 1-0.

In his entertaining diary of the season, Peter Reid gave his impression from the players' viewpoint:

'The crowd started going mad, cheering, stamping their feet, jumping up and down. The crowd were so ecstatic that I really thought Liverpool were getting beaten...I saw a lad with a radio in his ear and I went over and asked him and he said Liverpool were one-up, but it had been an exciting five minutes.'

The second half was one of the strangest experienced at the ground. The match was now played in almost surreal silence as the crowd waited anxiously for news of a comeback at Stamford Bridge. Although Everton required a Chelsea win, a draw may have been acceptable for the Hammers, whose last game may have been a potential title decider at Goodison on the Monday.

With Everton now having done their job, the home side visibly relaxed and Southampton were allowed several opportunities to get a goal back, but on 55 minutes a pin-point Sheedy cross was met perfectly by Graeme Sharp, whose typical towering header went wide of Grainger's right hand. Four minutes later the away side scored a consolation when Danny Wallace sped off from the halfway line and set up the substitute Puckett from close range.

But Lineker was not be a denied a hat-trick – two of which he would have gratefully swapped for the Manor Ground three days before – heading home after good work from Adrian Heath. But the Goodison patrons still had their ears on matters in London, and their subdued mood - disproving the old axiom that no news is good news - conveyed to the players that their efforts were in vain, and consequently the rest of the game was a tepid affair, apart from Jimmy Case causing a near brawl with a nasty lunge – and that's being kind - on Heath.

When the final whistle blew it was confirmed that Liverpool had clinched the title. The scenes were frankly unbelievable, as disconsolate players left the pitch with grown men in the crowd choking back the tears – and Everton had just won 6-1!

POSTSCRIPT:

Gary Lineker was a tormented soul after the game according to the *Daily Mirror*: 'Instead of a broad smile to go with the match ball to celebrate his fourth hat-trick, his face showed only bitter disappointment.' The England striker was philosophical; his comment that "I just wish I could swap a goal today for one against Oxford" was both predictable and depressing. Howard Kendall summed up the feeling of the 33,000 Evertonians present: "I've never felt so low after winning."

Everton would beat West Ham 3-1 at Goodison on the Monday to clinch the runners-up spot, for the first time since 1911-12. The less said about the rest the better. But in retrospect the 1985-86 league season was really the story of two matches that ended 2-1. After defeating Liverpool in February, the Blues went 11 points clear of their rivals by brushing aside Aston Villa at Goodison on the following Saturday, with Liverpool facing a tricky match at Spurs a day later. Lose or draw that and the deficit would be difficult to pull back with just 11 games left. But after trailing 1-0, a last-minute goal by Ian Rush clinched victory to at least keep the Reds in touch.

Although the Oxford match is cited as the night the title was lost, the crucial game for the Toffees was in truth at Luton in March. Leading 1-0 and in control on a miserably grey afternoon, instead of closing out the game in the manner they had become accustomed to, two uncharacteristically slack pieces of defending by Everton in the final 10 minutes gave the Hatters a 2-1 win. Howard Kendall admitted as much when he reflected on the season: "It was that game that disappointed me the most. We allowed Luton to score two from set pieces and lost ground." On the same day Liverpool drew level at the top.

The Southampton game was also the last in the refereeing career of Peter Willis, who made a habit of involving himself in vital days in Everton history. Willis of course sent off Kevin Moran in the 1985 FA Cup final, and he also dismissed Kevin Ratcliffe against Manchester City in the drawn quarter-final tie at Goodison in 1981 and then took charge of the replay which Everton lost 3-1, a defeat that effectively ended the reign of Gordon Lee and paved the way for Howard Kendall. On a happier note Willis was also in charge of the Chelsea game in April 1978 when Bob reached 30 league goals for the season.

As for 'Rumour Man', well the advances in modern technology have made him largely redundant. However 12 months later he would reappear at the climax of the 1986-87 season and this time he would bring only glad tidings. In the 1-0 win at Highbury in March, news was fed through to the away end that Wimbledon had gone ahead at Anfield and the scenes of jubilation came as a surprise to a young Neil Pointon in particular, as Howard Kendall confirmed on television that night: "Neil took a throw-in by the dugout and enquired why our supporters were cheering", said the Blues boss, "but he'll learn, he'll learn!"

As the Blues romped to the title in the spring, in three consecutive home matches against West Ham, Newcastle and Manchester City word got round, correctly this time, that Liverpool had conceded late winners. Cue mass celebrations everywhere, which at least helped erase the suffering of 12 months before.

But the final words on a strange day in May 1986 go to Ian Ross, then of the *Daily Post* and now Head of PR & External Affairs at Everton. 'Football will retain its position as sport's most intriguing game just as long as it continues to provide the sort of ludicrous scenarios witnessed at Goodison Park on Saturday.'

Gary Lineker fires home his second (top), while (above) the Blues traipse off, having just won 6-1...

Derek stings Hornets at both ends

Centre-half dominates game
Everton 3-2 Watford
First Division, 25th October, 1986

Players are meant to dominate games at one end of the pitch, either by scoring vital goals or making brilliant saves. Very occasionally one of the participants has an influence beyond the call of duty, dictating the result of the contest as a consequence of their actions in both areas.

The mention of Aston Villa's Chris Nicholl usually provokes a note of discord amongst Evertonians, as it was his speculative 30-yard shot that brought the Midlands team level in the 1977 League Cup final second replay. But it was his unique contribution to his team's cause at Filbert Street that provides the best example of the genre, for in the same season he was credited with all four goals in a 2-2 draw between Leicester and Villa. No Everton player can match that unique feat, but at Goodison against Watford in October 1986 Derek Mountfield certainly came close, and not for the first time against the Hornets.

Derek was a prodigious scorer of goals for a defender, with a record at Everton that only Stuart Pearce and Steve Bruce can match in the modern era - and they both took penalties. Although some were your typical defender's efforts from a set piece, others betrayed his earlier career as a forward, notably the poacher's goal against Ipswich at Goodison in the FA Cup. His 10 goals in 1984-85 remains the last time a defender reached double figures for the league season from open play.

The Blues went into the game in sixth place in the table, and welcomed back Neville Southall after an absence of seven months. Mountfield himself had missed most of the previous season and had only recently returned to the team following an injury to record signing Dave Watson. The Watford team included a swift return to Goodison for Kevin Richardson, who had left two months previously.

On a wet and windy afternoon the first half was typical of games at the time against the Vicarage Road outfit – plenty of effort but not one for the purists, with the ball frequently getting caught up in the swirling wind. 'The match was like playing ping-pong in a wind tunnel,' was the view of one journalist. Kevin Ratcliffe was nearly an unlikely marksman and Adrian Heath also went close on two occasions, with Luther Blissett shooting wide twice in the opening minutes for the visitors.

Things hotted up though in the second half, which kicked-off late as referee Mr Saville got lost inside the ground at half-time! A flurry of Everton corners led to Mountfield squeezing the ball home from close range on 52 minutes, after centre-half Steve Terry had failed to clear. But the tall defender had only two minutes to enjoy his moment of glory as he then sent John Barnes sprawling in the area after the England man weaved into the box. From the penalty spot Kenny Jackett gave Neville Southall no chance.

On the hour though Paul Power, who enjoyed an Indian summer that season, was tripped by full-back David Bardsley as he sped into the area. Typical of the game the resulting penalty had a touch of farce about it, and indeed ended up on *A Question of Sport* as a 'What Happened Next.' When Trevor Steven took the kick a photographer's groundsheet blew right in front of Watford keeper Sherwood, as the midfielder stuck the ball to his left. The referee ordered the penalty to be re-taken and Steven calmly put the ball again in exactly the same place. It was the only goal that afternoon that Mountfield was not involved in.

The Blues continued to be the classier team and, after several openings were squandered, it was a surprise that the Hornets got back into the game, thanks to that man Mountfield again. Substitute Lee Sinnott's long throw into the area could only be back-headed despairingly into his own net by the centre-half, which meant that the teams were now level with 12 minutes left. It was the second time in his career that Mountfield had scored at both ends in an Everton game, strangely the other instance was also against Watford, in the equally memorable 5-4 win in September 1984.

But his incredible day was far from over, and four minutes later he found the net for the third time in the game when heading powerfully home from a deep cross by Alan Harper. Watford pressed forward in search of an equalizer and Neville Southall's stoppage-time save to deny Mark Falco's header had a familiar ring to it.

POSTSCRIPT:

The Blues held on for a well-deserved victory and went on, of course, to Championship glory in May. The *Daily Mirror* reported that 'Derek Mountfield was still trying to decide whether or not his contribution to a bizarre afternoon came into the category of triumph or tragedy', whilst the star of the show was 'a bit peeved that they (the match officials) would not give me the match ball.'

Derek left for Aston Villa in 1988 where he continued in similar vein: against Norwich in the 1989-90 season he recorded own goals in both league games! He enjoyed many highlights in a successful career, but none were as memorable as this unusual *tour de force*.

Top: Paul Power is sent sprawling by David Bardsley in the area. Above: Derek Mountfield celebrates one of his two goals at the 'right end' for Everton

The future is not Orange

Blues tangoed
Luton Town 0-1 Everton
First Division, 2nd November, 1991

There have been a few unsavoury kits in the modern game (who can ever forget Coventry's fetching brown away kit of the late 1970s) and one that definitely fits into that class is Luton's orange away strip of the 1990s. Described by David Pleat as: "A bloody ridiculous kit, one of the director's wives must have chosen it," the strip was generally regarded as gruesome. But saying that, Everton should have a spot of affection for the much-maligned change kit - they had a 100% winning record when wearing it!

The background to this rather bizarre tale is a league match at Kenilworth Road in the 1991-92 season. Everton travelled south in mid-table and were coming into the game on the back of an excellent 4-1 League Cup win over Wolves. Luton were struggling, not even the presence of that one-man assault force Mick Harford up front or, indeed, a very young Mark Pembridge would prevent them going down at the end of the season. Making his home debut for Luton in this game was the one and only Chris Kamara.

The crowd and those in the press box were somewhat surprised to see Everton taking the field in the 'tasteless orange second strip' of their opponents. There was no explanation for the mystery, especially as the normal yellow away kit of the Toffees could have been worn with no problem. Some shirts plainly did not fit certain players.

The first hour of the match was lacklustre to say the least, with Ken Rogers of the *Liverpool Echo* musing: 'The bizarre mix-up over the colours seemed to have a psychological effect on the visitors. Not only did they look like Luton, they played like Luton.' Those in the executive boxes spent most of the time watching the Rugby Union World Cup final. Later Howard Kendall would say that he "felt sorry for people watching the first half."

It was only the arrival from the bench of Robert Warzycha on the hour that livened proceedings. The only point of interest up until then had been the propensity of the home side to kick the ball out of the ground, something they did six times in all during the course of the match!

After 65 minutes Peter Beagrie broke down the left and after beating two defenders (just the once each!) he pulled the ball back to Warzycha on the edge of the area and the Polish winger's shot was a real rocket, swerving away from Alec Chamberlain in the Luton goal. Two further chances fell to Atteveld and then Beagrie as the Blues - no, the Oranges - pressed home their advantage, but the away side held on and a 1-0 victory was a fair result.

POSTSCRIPT:

Howard Kendall was critical of his side: "We were unrecognizable in terms of our shirts and our performance in the first half." He also explained the kit mix-up: "The League Handbook states that Luton's shirts are predominantly white with blue trimmings, but in reality it is the opposite. The referee was right to demand a change, but we had not brought our yellow change strip and so we had to wear Luton's orange. It was annoying."

Despite the unfamiliar shirts, Robert Warzycha's strike was enough to defeat Luton Town

Find us keepers

Maine Road record
Manchester City 2-5 Everton
FA Premier League, 9th May, 1993

The first Premiership campaign of 1992-93 was an enigmatic one for the Blue half of Merseyside. For only the third time in history Everton won more matches away from home than at Goodison, with some exceptional performances - a 3-0 victory at Old Trafford and a derby win at home – being mixed with some that were dreadful, like the five-goal thrashing by QPR on Easter Monday. It was only a run of five wins out of seven in March that prevented an end-of-season relegation battle. Oh, and the form of a Geordie genius.

It was once said of Liam Brady when he was at Arsenal that in footballing terms he was tuned into the cultured sound of Radio 4, whilst his team-mates were struggling to find Radio 1. The same thing could have been said about Peter Beardsley with regard to most of his colleagues in the England international's two seasons at Everton.

By the time the Toffees journeyed to Maine Road on the final day the side were 15th in the table whilst City were sixth, with Peter Reid building on the success of the two previous seasons, which had seen fifth-place finishes in both.

One rule change for the start of the Premiership in 1992 was that clubs were granted dispensation to place a goalkeeper on the substitutes bench for all matches if they wished, as well as the usual two outfielders (although only two substitutes were allowed). Everton had already taken advantage of this change on two occasions, after Neville Southall had been sent off at QPR and Sheffield Wednesday. And it was this regulation that was to lead to a bit of football history at Maine Road.

City's problems began when their regular keeper Tony Coton injured himself in the pre-match warm-up - yes this does happen to other goalkeepers apart from Richard Wright - and Peter Reid decided to put the Welsh U21 international Martyn Margetson in his place. It was a decision both were to regret.

Just six minutes into the game a corner-kick from Andy Hinchcliffe was cleared as far as Beardsley, and Matt Jackson met his cross with a fine left-foot volley to put the visitors one-up. The former City man's corners were giving Margetson no end of problems and another viciously inswinging kick was punched out by the nervous keeper only as far as Peter Beagrie, who crashed a shot straight past the City goalkeeper.

Eleven minutes later and the City keeper had a lucky escape, this time he flapped at a near-post cross and the ball ran to Tony Cottee, who rammed the ball into the net. But, fortunately for the youngster, the linesman had flagged for offside. Three minutes later and Margetson's day got even worse, this time his attempted clearance went straight to Preki and although the Serb shot against the woodwork, Peter Beardsley was on hand to knock in the rebound. It was the England international's first goal from open play since January – and it was his final one for the club before his departure to Newcastle. (Beardsley himself once endured a nightmare game as a keeper for Newcastle at West Ham in April 1986, conceding three in an 8-1 defeat after their regular stopper Martin Thomas was injured. On reporting for England duty later that week he was jokingly issued with gloves and told to train with the keepers.)

Whilst City were being routed on the pitch, off it the home spectators entertained themselves by pelting the City chairman with eggs, with Howard Kendall - who had left Maine Road for Goodison three years before in controversial circumstances - also being in the firing line. Margetson was also understandably the target for abuse from the terraces, and there was the unusual sight of replacement keeper Andy Dibble, on his birthday, being cheered as he warmed up on the sidelines. Six minutes before the break David White at least gave the home fans some solace by heading in Rick Holden's corner.

City had a foothold back in the game at half-time, but such was the nightmare endured by young Margetson that Peter Reid had no option but to replace him during the break. The Welshman allegedly drove straight home (it was a bad afternoon for Welsh U21 keepers as Danny Coyne, who was Margetson's international understudy, was sent off after just 38 minutes of his Tranmere debut at Peterborough).

Dibble's clean sheet for the afternoon lasted just six minutes in fact, as Preki fired a real cracker from 20 yards for his second of the game. Just after the hour we had the unusual sight though of a fourth keeper in the match, as Jason Kearton replaced Neville Southall in the Everton net. It was the first time any game had featured substitute goalkeepers for both teams. You had to go back 98 years for an Everton match with four keepers, when the Toffees used three at Sheffield United.

Ten minutes later City made it 4-2 with a penalty after Hinchcliffe handled a cross in the box. Curle's successful spot-kick also meant all four keepers had conceded goals as well, which must be some sort of record. But the away side were to have the final word when with six minutes left Peter Beagrie drove home powerfully from 20 yards for a well-deserved victory. He celebrated with the now traditional somersaults. Following on from Preki's howitzer the *Manchester Evening News* made the point that: 'Even if Margetson and Dibble had both been between the sticks together they would have been powerless to prevent Everton rubbing salt into the wounds with these two magnificent strikes.'

POSTSCRIPT:

Howard Kendall was pleased with the final act of the campaign: "We wanted to finish on a winning note. You never like your last league game to be a disappointing one, because you have all summer to think about it." The boot was on the other foot 11 years later when an end-of-season defeat at City would leave Everton with some serious soul-searching.

The Everton boss also spoke about the missile attack. "Yes, I was hit by eggs, but I don't want to make a big deal about it", before adding humorously "you would have thought that Dave Watson, with all his experience, would have known better than to sit next to me here!"

The *Manchester Evening News* protested that: 'Saturday's horror show against Howard Kendall's side must rank as the most abject display from a City side in Reid's time in the hot seat.' Peter Reid was equally bemused: "That was the worst performance since I have been manager and it leaves me wondering a few things about my players." Unfortunately for Everton's midfield maestro, he didn't have long to ponder – after three consecutive top-10 finishes, he was disgracefully sacked four months later, after just four games in charge at the start of the 1993-94 season.

And what happened to Martyn Margetson, who made a major contribution to the day's entertainment? The Welshman had ironically been given his City debut by Howard Kendall in October 1990, and this match was his first appearance of the campaign. He played 57 times for Manchester City and at the start of the 2006-07 season he was at Cardiff City.

When did 19 Everton players appear in the same game?

Three years before the 5-2 win the Toffees had gone to Maine Road, in April 1990. Howard Kendall had been manager of City for four months at that time and to shore things up he had surrounded himself with players who had served him proud at Goodison in the mid-80s. So in the game against Everton the following players appeared in the City line-up: Alan Harper, Peter Reid, Adrian Heath,Wayne Clarke, as well as Gary Megson, Andy Hinchcliffe and Mark Ward. Of the 25 players used in the game, no fewer than 19 played for Everton during their careers.

Top: Peter Beardsley's challenges City skipper Keith Curle, while above Preki rifles home Everton's fourth goal from long range

Segers Hans it to the Blues

The game that would not go away
Everton 3-2 Wimbledon
FA Premier League, 7th May, 1994

T he main problem with discussing this memorable match is just where to start. What about Barry Horne's screamer? Anders Limpar's, er, two–and-a-half with full pike in the box? Or the Swede's pretensions as a volleyball player? Or Gary Ablett's shank? And as for the winner, well that was worthy of a whole book in itself. Which is exactly what happened.

Everton started the day third-from-bottom, and there were more permutations than an average *National Lottery* draw for those in and around the drop-zone. Paradoxically for the Toffees, a draw might have been enough to keep them up, but they could still be relegated with a victory. On the morning of possibly the most important game in the club's history, the table looked like this:

17.	Southampton	42 (GD -17)
18.	Sheff Utd	42 (-17)
19.	Ipswich	42 (-23)
---	-----------	-----------
20.	Everton	41 (-20)
21.	Oldham	39 (-26)
22.	Swindon	30

With Swindon already gone, the others at the bottom had certainly picked the right season to be involved in a relegation dog-fight. Only 12 months earlier Crystal Palace had unbelievably gone down with no less than 49 points.

The lead-up to the encounter only added to the atmosphere of intrigue and anticipation around the big day. One or two of the Wimbledon players revealed that they were not exactly enamoured of playing at Goodison with the stakes being so high for the home team. Warren Barton let slip that: "It's not the nicest of places to go to - especially with the situation as it is, that they could go down. That is one thing that has crossed our minds. They are football fanatics up there." The Dons' suspicions were borne out when, in the early hours of the morning of the game, their coach was torched outside the team hotel in Warrington. Although there was a police investigation, Everton chief executive Jim Greenwood was keen to distance the club from such an unsavoury event: "Everton fans have proved over the years that they know how to behave in all circumstances." But the incident had an unsettling effect on the visitors.

The other big story concerned the marathon takeover wrangle involving Peter Johnson, one that was resolved just two days before the big game when the then Tranmere chairman took control after agreeing to underwrite a £10m share issue. Bill Kenwright was a relieved man. "I have been desperately keen for this whole issue to be resolved. Now all we want is the right result on Saturday to ensure we can channel our new resources into making a major impact in the top-flight next season."

Meanwhile Everton manager Mike Walker spoke candidly about the match: "There isn't another game after tomorrow. This is it. This is our last chance. Everybody is aware of that - me, the players and the fans." With echoes of Southampton in 1986, there was no greater metaphor to show how Everton's fortunes had slipped than supporters, who eight years earlier had been glued to their radios waiting for news on fellow title challengers, and would now be listening with some trepidation for updates concerning fellow relegation candidates. If it was not good then the football equivalent of Armageddon beckoned.

The day dawned fine and warm, and the reduced capacity (due to the reconstruction of the Park End) combined with the fact that the game was not all-ticket meant that queues started early, and the gates were locked with 31,000 inside the ground before kick-off. It is, and will probably remain, the smallest capacity crowd in Goodison's history.

Walker included all four strikers in the squad, with Cottee and Rideout starting whilst Angell and Barlow were on the bench. Wimbledon had enjoyed a fine season - they were sixth when the match started - and were in the middle of a purple patch under Joe Kinnear when they were not a bad footballing team: any side with players such as Scales, Barton, Earle and Holdsworth had to command respect. But the presence of a certain Vincent Jones, who had been sent off at Goodison in his two previous appearances for the club, acted as a reminder of the bad old days.

The start could not have been worse - a corner from the Everton right by Gary Elkins was handled quite inexplicably by Anders Limpar, and referee Robbie Hart had little option but to award a penalty that was converted by Dean Holdsworth, despite a brave effort by Neville Southall. On 20 minutes came the moment that surely condemned the home team to relegation, when a mix-up between Unsworth and Watson was followed by a comical slice by Gary Ablett into his own net.

But dramatically Everton were back into the match just four minutes later, after Anders Limpar, 'whose plunge was so theatrical it must have impressed the watching Bill Kenwright' did enough to convince the referee that some sort of actual bodily harm had been inflicted in the Wimbledon area. Graham Stuart had volunteered to take any penalties, although he may not have been so keen if he had known that, earlier in the season, Hans Segers had saved three Liverpool penalties at Selhurst Park (one in normal time and two in a penalty shootout). In 1989 the Dutchman had also saved a Graeme Sharp penalty in a FA Cup match at Goodison. But 'Diamond' kept his nerve and the home team were in with a shout.

Just afterwards came a moment that would shape not only the match but Everton's fortunes for years to come. A cross from the left gave Dean Holdsworth a gilt-edged opportunity but he contrived to head just over when unmarked from six yards out. Had that gone in then Everton's history since 1994 may have read quite different. As it was Everton went in just one goal down at half-time, although results elsewhere confirmed the view that a victory was still needed.

The second half followed much the same pattern as the first, plenty of huff-and-puff from the home team with the visitors creating the more meaningful chances. And then it was a case of cometh the hour, cometh the man.

These days Barry Horne may rightly enjoy heroic status amongst Everton supporters, but up until 4.25pm on Saturday 7th May 1994 it was fair to say he had been one of the more obvious targets for criticism from disgruntled fans. After a debut goal against Sheffield Wednesday, the Welsh international, with typical modesty, proclaimed: "Don't hold your breath waiting for the second." Nearly two years later Barry waited for the perfect moment for his next strike. After shrugging off the challenge of Vinnie Jones he struck a thunderbolt from 30 yards out that flew past the despairing dive of Hans Segers. All the same the job was only half done, as at that point, if results had stayed the same, the table would have looked like this:

| 17. Southampton | 45 |
| 18. Sheff Utd | 45 |
19. Ipswich	43
20. Everton	42
21. Oldham	42
22. Swindon	30

Horne was close to a second goal until, with just nine minutes left, came the Everton winner that preserved the Toffees' top-flight status, although it would have repercussions that would be felt for many years after. Graham Stuart played a one-two with Cottee on the edge of the box and his first-time shot appeared to take Segers by surprise, the keeper allowing the ball to bounce over his arms and into the net. Nine minutes of sheer torture followed, as the home team kept the visitors at bay to hold out for a victory that, although scarcely deserved, was probably the most important in the history of the club.

POSTSCRIPT:

The mass of relieved and frenzied supporters on the pitch at the end of the game told its own story. After the dust had settled Oldham went down with Swindon whilst a last-minute Mark Stein goal at Stamford Bridge relegated Sheffield United as well (ironically their manager Dave Bassett had sent two crates of champagne to Wimbledon on the Friday night as an incentive).

Whilst Mike Walker saluted the home fans, Joe Kinnear was rueing a missed opportunity, as Sam Hammam had promised the team a trip to Las Vegas if they had avoided defeat. The Wimbledon boss blamed the arson-related 5.15am alarm call at the hotel, and joked: "There's one good thing about losing - we'll get out of here with our lives intact. If we'd won we would have stayed until Monday." As for the winner, he claimed: "I could have saved the third goal", before adding: "I think Segers has a few relatives up here." Those comments were to have a greater significance than had been realised at the time.

Regina v Segers

The Everton vWimbledon game should have been consigned to the history books as a memorable - if slightly embarrassing, given the circumstances - Goodison occasion. But the rumours that surrounded the game ensured that the fixture would simply not be forgotten in a hurry.

On Wednesday 9th November 1994, *The Sun* published details of an alleged match-fixing 'sting' involving Bruce Grobbelaar. When Fleet Street had got word that a bribery scandal was about to hit the news-stalls, the general consensus was that it would concern the game at Goodison in May. In his compelling account of the whole saga, *Foul Play*, journalist David Thomas described how, on the preceding Tuesday, Sam Hammam (who was a friend of Bill Kenwright) had denied any wrongdoing and pointed to the incentive to the players of the holiday to Las Vegas. For his part, in his book *The Final Score*, Hans Segers described being phoned on the same day by two journalists who both inquired whether he knew about any footballers being offered bribes. On Saturday 12th November, Segers then raised the subject of the rumours surrounding the game to the press: 'For a few crazy hours on Tuesday, people had been ringing my home, asking if it was me.'

On 14th March 1995, Hans Segers was arrested in connection with the allegations and on 24th July 1995 he was one of five people charged under Section One of the Criminal Act, 1977, '...to give and corruptly to accept gifts of money as inducements improperly to influence the outcome of football matches or as rewards for having done so.'

The case of Regina v Lim, Fashanu, Segers, Grobbelaar commenced on 14th January 1997. In court, Segers was questioned about a Swiss bank account, containing £160,000. David Calvert-Smith, for the prosecution, described seven payments into this account during 1993 and 1994, all during or just after the football season. One of those highlighted was an amount of £19,000 paid in on 13th May 1994, six days after the visit to Goodison. Calvert-Smith also gave details of phone traffic between Segers, John Fashanu and their associate Paul Lim, both before and just after the match.

In his defence, Segers maintained that the money in the account came from several sources: from Fashanu for a joint-business venture, from a tie business he was involved in and for forecasting the results of Dutch football matches for Paul Lim. He also explained that these were the reasons for the phone calls. When shown tapes of 19 Wimbledon matches (that Calvert-Smith stated may have been thrown) by his defence barrister, Desmond de Silva, Segers denied any wrongdoing. With regard to the Stuart goal, Segers elaborated in court: 'I am not sure who scored. He hit a shot and I dived. I had it covered all the way, but it hit a divot, popped up and changed direction.' Bob Wilson had been called as a witness for the defence, and he could find nothing questionable in any of the videotape evidence.

On Tuesday 1st March the jury gave their verdict against all the defendants: they were deadlocked. There would need to be a retrial. The 'replay' took place in the summer of 1997 and, after much deliberation, Segers was found not guilty. He is now currently goalkeeping coach at Tottenham Hotspur.

Top: Neville Southall fails to keep out Dean Holdsworth's early penalty, and things look bleak. Above: Graham Stuart (partially hidden) somehow finds the net to complete Everton's comeback

A half of two games
Pre-season oddity
Everton 2-0 Espanyol
Everton 0-0 Standard Liege
Le Tournoi de Gala, 2nd August, 1998

❛ Le Tournoi de Gala' was a rather strange pre-season tournament involving three clubs, staged on a single day at Slessin, Liege. It was to be contested on a round-robin basis, where each played the other two in matches of 45 minutes duration. The way of calculating points was so complex, only somebody working for NASA could have devised it.

What made the occasion even more unusual was that Everton had actually played a 90-minute friendly in Alkmaar over the border in Holland the day before, where they had failed to impress in a 3-1 defeat despite giving debuts to Olivier Dacourt and Marco Materazzi. When they arrived in Belgium, Everton touched unlucky, being drawn to play in the opening two matches so they had a break of only an hour between their games.

The first match was against Espanyol, with the Blues fielding only three of the starting line-up that had played in Holland 24 hours before. The 6,000 crowd were treated to a goal inside the first minute, in fact there was just 53 seconds on the clock when Don Hutchison's cross was turned past his own keeper by left-back Nando. Within four minutes Everton were two-up, a cross from Tony Thomas was mis-kicked by Dacourt back to the defender, and this time his centre was met perfectly by John Spencer, whose volley went in off the post.

Even though it was a friendly, the match was highly competitive with Everton forgetting their poor display of the previous day to dictate the pattern of play, although near the end of the 45 minutes tempers frayed and two players were booked, one being Michael Ball.

After their break the Toffees returned to play Standard Liege. (Incidentally the best, and probably the only, anecdote about Liege concerns the former Leeds chairman Leslie Silver. When Leeds were drawn against the Belgian club in Europe, he returned to Elland Road and told the players: 'Right lads, we've been drawn against Standard Liege – and the first leg is in Standard.'

He was supposed to be the brains of the outfit.)

Only five of the Everton side retained their starting place in front of a crowd that had now grown to 10,000, although the match was surprisingly a low-key affair in contrast to the opening game. Liege had most of the pressure, with the only point of interest being the introduction for the Blues of the Tunisian trialist Yasser El Hamruunin, for the second 'half' of the half. He was unable to make much of an impression as both teams struggled in a game that ended goalless.

Under the rules of the competition, a drawn game would be decided by penalties and Everton, in typical fashion, blew the shootout and lost 3-2 thanks to misses by Tony Grant, John Spencer and Don Hutchison. The final game saw Liege and Espanyol battle out another 0-0 draw, with the Belgian club again triumphing in the penalty contest.

But thanks to the rather perverse way in which the points were calculated - three for a win, one for a draw and an additional point if victorious in a penalty shootout - Everton found themselves as victors, with their win and a draw counting for four points, with Liege also netting four points thanks to two draws and two penalty shootout wins, but the two goals against Espanyol gave the Toffees the edge. Confused?

Marco Materazzi - An Everton debutant in August 1998

The strangest game I have ever seen

A Goodison epic
Everton 1-0 Blackburn Rovers
Barclays Premiership, 11th February 2006

Those lucky to have been at Goodison for Everton's sixth home match of 2006 saw a game that will live long in the memory. It was a game with everything: unrelenting drama and passion, one of the great Goodison misses, disallowed goals aplenty, a peculiar dismissal and a bit of goalkeeping history. And that was the opening half-hour! It was a draining experience, even for the most seasoned of football watchers.

The Blues had been beaten at Chelsea in the FA Cup in the midweek before the game and had also lost goalkeeper Richard Wright to the now infamous collision with a board in the goalmouth before the match (Nigel Martyn had succumbed to a persistant ankle problem that would force the keeper to end his career in summer 2006). Iain Turner had made his debut in that match and he retained his place for the game against the Lancashire side, who were going well under Mark Hughes. John Ruddy was recalled from a loan spell at Darlington to take his place on the bench. They were effectively the Toffees' third and fourth keepers.

Rovers started the game well but after five minutes James Beattie broke the offside trap and his flick-on was turned past Brad Friedel by Tim Cahill, but the Australian was adjudged to be marginally offside. Within 60 seconds there was an amazing moment when a collision between Friedel and Lucas Neill gave James McFadden what was basically a free shot at an open goal from 10 yards, but the Scot slammed his shot against the underside of the bar. (This was one of the worst misses seen by the author at Goodison, but ranks behind one perpetrated by Paul Gascoigne for Newcastle at the Gwladys Street End in March 1988, Gazza striking the underside of the bar when presented with an open goal from a distance that would be more appropriately measured in inches rather than feet.)

What was developing into a game with a slightly unusual feel then turned surreal. A misplaced header by Alan Stubbs resulted in Turner being caught in 'no man's land' just outside his area and the young keeper instinctively reached down and handled, leaving referee Philip Walton no alternative than to dismiss the Premiership debutant - although subsequent analysis would show that it was doubtful whether a goalscoring opportunity had been denied. So on comes John Ruddy, at 19 years and four months Everton's youngest keeper for 30 years, for his Toffees debut. This begged the obvious question: when was the last occasion before this match that two goalkeepers made their league debut for the same club in the same game?

The game amazingly was just nine minutes old at this stage. After 16 minutes Everton had another goal disallowed when Cahill's header was said to have been from an offside position. The atmosphere bordered on the frenzied as the home crowd fervently backed the players, who responded brilliantly, continuing to belie the disadvantage of being a man short as they pinned Rovers back, and they were rewarded for their efforts when a quickly taken free-kick from the right by Mikel Arteta was brilliantly anticipated by Beattie, and his header flashed past Friedel.

The second half saw more of the same as Everton pressed forward - with Arteta and Beattie particularly impressing - whilst at the back the young debutant keeper was protected by a steely defence. Ten minutes into the second half and Everton had their third goal disallowed, this time for a foul by Beattie as Stubbs headed in at the Gwladys Street End.

With half-an-hour left Blackburn began to press home their numerical advantage and nearly equalized when Michael Gray's header went over Ruddy and was headed out from under the crossbar by Stubbs. Robbie Savage the sent a shot just over the bar and Ruddy saved well from Florent Sinama-Pongolle and Sergio Peter. With 10 minutes left Lee Carsley came on for Beattie, who left the field to a standing ovation after one of the bravest centre-forward performances seen at Goodison for many years.

As the game entered the final throes Blackburn threw everyone forward, including Friedel for corner-kicks and it was from one of these that the ball fell to Cahill and, with the keeper stranded, the Australian's shot from inside his own half was fired wide. If that had gone in then that would have set the seal on a remarkable afternoon.

POSTSCRIPT:

At the final whistle the partisan crowd celebrated the win like a Cup final, but the final word goes to a wise old sage from the Goodison press box: 'In 50 years of watching football here that's the strangest game I have ever seen.'

Other Everton keeper dismissals

Gordon West v Newcastle United (a), 28th October 1967

The first, and possibly the most infamous of the five dismissals. The league game at Newcastle 'boiled over into a shambles' according to the *Liverpool Echo*. After Ollie Burton had been sent off for a foul on Alex Young, two minutes from time West made a fine save and as he released the ball there was a 'bit of a skirmish' with Albert Bennett being 'laid out' (as described earlier, Bennett himself had been one of two Newcastle players dismissed in a particularly violent reserve match against the Blues in 1966). The linesman brought the incident to the attention of the referee, who dismissed the Everton goalkeeper. Substitute Sandy Brown, on for Johnny Morrissey, went in goal and he had no chance from Jim Iley's spot-kick. It was the only goal of the game.

Neville Southall v Chelsea (a), 12th October 1985

See Match 42, page 201.

Neville Southall v QPR (a), 28th December 1992

Seven years later and the great man is one of two players dismissed - Paul Rideout was the other - in a 4-2 defeat. After 20 minutes a back-pedalling Dave Watson heads it back to the keeper who instinctively handles just outside the box, and Gerald Ashby has no alternative under FIFA regulations other than to red card the Everton keeper. 'If that is the law, the law is an ass' was the view of one of the press.

Other Everton keeper dismissals (cont)

Neville Southall v Sheffield Wednesday (a), 6th February 1993

Remarkably Nev has another early bath just six weeks later. With Everton already 2-0 down he handles Paul Warhurst's shot when just outside the box and is dismissed. Substitute Jason Kearton is powerless to stop a 3-1 defeat.

Career clean sheet

Recognised Everton keepers who have never conceded a goal in a first-team match:

90 minutes

John Patrick	v Burnley (h),	28th November 1896
Dick Depledge	v Stoke City (h),	16th March 1907
Mike Stowell	v Millwall (h - Simod Cup),	20th December 1988

81 minutes

John Ruddy	v Blackburn Rovers (h),	11th February 2006

Tim Cahill ponders the offside decision which cost him a goal (above, left). Iain Turner is dismissed nine minutes into the match, with the referee earning a 'thumbs-up' from Blackburn's on-loan Liverpool forward Florent Sinama-Pongolle

Above: James Beattie meets Mikel Arteta's quick free-kick to head the winner against Blackburn Rovers

Above, left: Celebrations following James Beattie's goal. Above, right: Manager David Moyes congratulates debutant John Ruddy at the end of the match

Other titles produced by Sport Media:

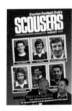

Sport Media
A Trinity Mirror Business

All of these titles are available to order by calling 0845 143 0001, or you can buy online at www.merseyshop.com